Nigerian Dwarf Goat

Nigerian Dwarf Goats as pets.

Nigerian Dwarf Goat book for pros and cons, housing, keeping, diet and health.

By

Macy Peterson

ALL RIGHTS RESERVED. This book contains material protected under International and Federal Copyright Laws and Treaties.

Any unauthorized reprint or use of this material is strictly prohibited. No part of this book may be reproduced or transmitted in any form or by any means, electronic, mechanical or otherwise, including photocopying or recording, or by any information storage and retrieval system without express written permission from the author.

Copyright © 2018

Published by: Zoodoo Publishing

Table of Contents

Table of Contents 3

Introduction 4

Chapter 1: Understanding a Nigerian dwarf goat 7

Chapter 2: Owning a Nigerian dwarf goat 21

Chapter 3: Decoding the Nigerian dwarf goat's behaviour 33

Chapter 4: Setting up the Nigerian dwarf goat's home 38

Chapter 5: Breeding and Reproduction in Nigerian dwarf goats 51

Chapter 6: Diet requirements of the Nigerian dwarf goat 66

Chapter 7: Health of the Nigerian dwarf goat 75

Chapter 8: Grooming the Nigerian dwarf goat 94

Chapter 9: Training the Nigerian dwarf goat 100

Conclusion 107

References 109

Introduction

I want to thank you and congratulate you for buying the book 'Nigerian dwarf goat as a pet'. This book will help you to understand everything you need to know about domesticating a Nigerian dwarf goat. You will learn all the aspects related to raising the Nigerian dwarf goat successfully at home. You will be able to understand the pros and cons, behaviour, basic care, keeping, housing, diet and health related to the animal.

There are people who are impressed by the adorable looks of the Nigerian dwarf goat. They think that this reason is enough to domesticate the animal. But, domestication of a Nigerian dwarf goat has its unique challenges and issues.

If you are not ready for these challenges, then you are not ready to domesticate the animal. If you have already bought or adopted a Nigerian dwarf goat, even then you need to understand your pet so that you take care of him in a better way. It is important that you understand that owning any pet will have its advantages and disadvantages.

You should see whether with all its pros and cons, the animal fits well into your household. Domesticating and taming a pet is not only fun. There is a lot of hard work that goes into it. It is important that you are ready to commit before you decide to domesticate the animal. If you are a prospective buyer, then understanding of these points will help you to make a wise decision.

When you bring a pet home, it becomes your responsibility to raise the pet in the best way possible. You have to provide physically, mentally, emotionally and financially for the pet. Before you embark on this journey of raising your pet, it is important to evaluate your resources and make sure that you are ready for the pet. You should also evaluate the practical side of things. It is important that you know that the cost of bringing up a Nigerian dwarf goat might be more than the cost you would have to encounter while raising a dog or a cat.

It is important to have a thorough understanding about the animal. Spend some time to know everything about the Nigerian dwarf goat. This will help you know your pet better. The more you know about your pet, the better bond you will form with him. Whenever you get a pet home, you have to make sure that you are all ready for the responsibilities ahead. A pet is like a family member. This is the basic requirement to domesticate an animal. It is more than important that you take care of all the responsibilities for the animal.

If you wish to raise a Nigerian dwarf goat as a pet, there are many things that you need to keep in mind. It can get very daunting for a new owner. Because of the lack of information, you will find yourself getting confused as to what should be done and what should be avoided. You might be confused and scared. But, there is no need to feel so confused. After you learn about the Nigerian dwarf goats, you will know how adorable they are. You should equip yourself with the right knowledge.

It is important that you understand the basic behaviour of the Nigerian dwarf goat. This will help you to understand what lies ahead of you. If you understand how a Nigerian dwarf goat should be cared for, you will make it work for yourself. You should aim at learning about the animal and then doing the right thing for him. This will help you to form a relationship with him.

Once you form a relationship with the Nigerian dwarf goat, it gets better and easier for you as the owner. The pet will grow up to be friendly and adorable. He will also value the bond as much as you do. This will be good for the pet and also for you as the pet owner in the long run.

If you are in two minds whether you need a Nigerian dwarf goat or not, then this book will make it simpler for you. You should objectively look at the various advantages and disadvantages of owning a Nigerian dwarf goat. This will help you to make your decision. If you are looking to domesticate the Nigerian dwarf goat, then you might be having many questions and doubts. You still might not be sure whether you want to buy the Nigerian dwarf goat or not. If you are still doubtful, then this book is meant to help you make a well-informed decision.

This book is meant to equip you with all the knowledge that you need to have before buying the Nigerian dwarf goat and bringing it home. This book will help you understand the basic behaviour and antics of the animal. You will also learn various tricks and tips. These tips and tricks will be a quick guide when you are looking for different ways to have fun with your pet. It is important that a prospective buyer has all the important information regarding a Nigerian dwarf goat.

You need to make sure that you are ready in terms of the right preparation. This book will help you in this preparation and be a better owner for your pet. You will learn many ways to take care of your Nigerian dwarf goat. This book will try to address every question that you might have when looking at raising the Nigerian dwarf goat. You will be able to understand the pet and give it the care that it requires.

You can expect to learn the pet's basic behaviour, eating habits, shelter requirements, grooming and training techniques among other important things. In short, the book will help you to be a better owner by learning everything about the animal. This will help you form an everlasting bond with the pet.

Chapter 1: Understanding a Nigerian dwarf goat

Usually, the first question that comes up is why anyone would want a Nigerian dwarf goat. And, the second concern is if these are regular sized goats with some genetic or developmental defects. To learn more about these two common queries we will have to take a peek into the history of livestock and their association with people.

If you are seriously considering having goats as pets, then you must prepare yourself for a great deal of responsibility that is about to come your way. Of course, goats are really gentle and quite cute. They make wonderful pets and can be really rewarding farm animals, too.

However, the most important thing that you need to understand when you are bringing home a pet goat is that this animal needs special care and attention. Yes, the regular pets like cats and dogs need the same amount of care. However, the advantage that you have with these conventional pets is that you have enough support and also a lot of information available about the health and care of these animals.

1. What is a Nigerian dwarf goat?

If you are looking to domesticate this unique animal then it is critical that you make an effort to understand what a Nigerian dwarf goat is. A breed of goat that is much smaller in size and weight as compared to other goats is known as a Nigerian dwarf goat.

The Nigerian Dwarf Goat is one of the two miniature goat breeds that are reared by goat lovers across the globe. This is a breed of African origin that has become popular because of its ability to live comfortably in the urban set up.

These goats can be really attached to their owners. When you bottle raise these goats, they can be exceptionally clingy, which is bittersweet in a way. While you love the fact that they are so close and bonded, you will find them following you.

There are many other breeds of the Nigerian dwarf goats that are derived by cross breeding between the available and popular breeds.

2. Difference between the Nigerian dwarf goat and normal sized goat?

Many a times, prospective owners wonder whether the only difference between the Nigerian dwarf goat and the large sized goats is the size of the animals. It should be noted here that there are many other features that can help distinguish a micro and other goats.

The ears of the Nigerian dwarf goat are very small in size. These ears are perked back in their appearance. The back of the goat is known to be swayed in appearance.

This is what makes them stand out in comparison to other goats that are normal sized. The entire look of the goat is very chubby if you care to look carefully. The goat has a compact body and curved profile. Its legs are short and rounded.

3. A brief history

In the West African region, a certain breed of goat known as the West African Dwarf was predominant. These goats were distributed across Africa but were concentrated in the Senegal region in Central region and Southern Sudan.

These goats were descendants of the Central African species. The small stature of the goat was due to a type of dwarfism. The dwarfism in the pygmy goats led to shorter and plumper bodies. They also had a short head and short legs. This condition was called achondroplasia. Another type of dwarfism called pituitary hypoplasia led to smaller goats that had normal proportions.

This breed was used mostly for its meat and for the production of milk. Of course, in these regions, these goats were not really kept as pets for obvious economic reasons. Back then, these breeds were not really cultivated or grown in large numbers. They mostly thrived according to the "survival of the fittest" principal.

According to the documents of Albert Schweitzer, this breed of goat was used to provide milk to the hospital. The advantage with this breed was that it was immune to the Tse Tse fly. While most imported breeds were unable to survive this fly, the pygmy goat remained productive.

How these goats reached America has several stories associated with it. The most widely accepted story is that these goats were shipped along with big cats to America. The cats were meant to be displayed at the zoos. The goats were primarily meant to be food for these large cats. The goats that were not eaten by the cats were taken to the zoo, too.

For a long time, even the Nigerian Dwarf Goats were referred to as Pygmy Goats. It was only when the breeders recognised the stark differences between the breeds that they understood that there were two unique breeds that existed. While one was stocky, the other was lean.

These observations were shared globally and all the breeder agreed upon the differences. A lady named Mrs. Bonnie Abrahamson, who worked in a zoo in California is credited with noticing the difference between the two breeds.

She coined the name Nigerian Dwarves and brought several such black and white goats to the Pygmy Certification Committee. They were accepted in the herdbook. However, a similar variety that was found in Indiana was rejected because it was brown in colour.

That is when a petition was sent to the International Dairy Goat Registry to open a separate book for the Nigerian Dwarves. In the year 1981, the first buck was included into this book with defined characteristics. In just 6 years from then, there were about 384 goats in the list.

These goats were mostly found in black, brown and gold colours. Initially, the breeders tried hard to keep these colours exclusive. However, due to the limited variations, these goats were mixed to create newer colour variations

With these developments and with better facilities of transport and refrigeration, larger goats began to gain popularity. While the whole world was shifting towards large sized livestock, there were some who were still researching about the smaller breeds and methods to produce healthy specimens of these breeds.

In the late 1960s, breeding of smaller livestock was started by a Mexican rancher. He admitted that he wanted to create miniature livestock as pets for those who could afford it. He then partnered with a veterinary researcher and shifted the focus of the project towards producing more on a smaller piece of land. This drew the interest of several organizations across the world, the most noteworthy one being the US National Research Council.

Then, a Texan breeder noticed that the size of the goats and livestock on the show ring was steadily on the rise. So, he decided to start a program to downsize the Hereford Livestock in the 1970s. This breed hails from Herefordshire in England. The goal of this breeder was to produce specimens that were smaller in size but excellent in their conformation.

Simultaneously, a research project was being conducted in Australia. This project that went on from 1974 to 1993 was primarily focused on dwarfing if the smaller specimens of livestock were more efficient in producing meat. This led to the production of the Lowline breed. This breed was used as the closed herd of small sized livestock in this project. The efficiency was the same as the larger goats and thus, the interest in this breed continued, allowing them to survive.

In Seattle, Washington, around the same time, breeders Arlene Gradwohl and Richard Gradwohl noticed that urbanization was happening quickly. There were several housing developments that began to mushroom around the area. Being a farm man himself, Richard wanted to make sure that he was able to retain the rural lifestyle. He had a background as a business professor and he began to research about the commercial value of the possible opportunities to maintain farm life.

He realized that smaller livestock had greater value on smaller property. Since he advocated innovation, he began his research on miniature livestock and acquired livestock and learnt line-breeding techniques. Then he got extremely interested in developing new breeds of these Nigerian dwarf goats. He has developed almost 18 new breeds of miniature livestock.

It is true that the third world countries and other developing nations still maintain interest in the larger breeds. But several farm owners have realized that it is futile to pursue larger livestock. In fact, during the 1980's research conducted by the National Research Council helped raise awareness in almost 80 countries about the potential of miniature livestock. This, they claimed would actually help develop these nations.

4. Life span of Nigerian dwarf goats

A Nigerian dwarf goat has a life span of 12-14 years. It is known that a goat that is cared for and groomed in a good way will have a long life span. The key is to provide them with the right environment and also the right nutrition. This will help them to grow, stay healthy and live longer.

5. Body structure

The body of the goat must be levelled and long. As the animal ages, bowing may occur. This is acceptable. The shoulder blades or the withers must be very sharp and defined. The points must be slightly above the level of the back.

It is important for the ribs to be long and wide. They must be spaced well and must be well sprung as well. This gives the body cavity the shape that is desired.

The body cavity must be proportional. It is deep and has ample room for all the internal organs. The rumen also has a good capacity to help during pregnancy. The chest floor is wide and the legs are widely placed, too. When you look at the body from a top angle, it must appear wedge shaped.

6. Size, colour and weight

In comparison to the other miniature varieties of goats, which is the Pygmy Goat, the Nigerian Dwarf Goat is a tad smaller. The size of a Nigerian Goat is measured from the toes up to the withers.

This height is usually about 16 to 19 inches. Of course, they can grow to a maximum height of about 22 inches for the bucks and 21 inches for the does.

As for Nigerian Dwarf Goats, there is no such thing as a minimum size. This is probably because of the slow growth of the Dwarf Goats. They tend to grow faster when they are older.

These standards show us that miniature livestock start off really small. The weight of the livestock varies from one breed to another. The standards are an average measurement to determine if a specimen is healthy or not. If you are solely into hobby breeding and farming, a few inches of deviation from standards will not matter.

However, in case of miniature livestock shows, it is imperative to stick to the standards that have been established for specific breeds in order to qualify to showcase your livestock.

There are three colour lines that are accepted for Nigerian Dwarf Goats. These colours include: Black, Brown and Gold.

The goat may have a solid coat colour in one of the shades. It is also acceptable to have combinations of these main colours in the body of the goat. Usually, the solid colours have sharp demarcations of the contrasting colours. These markings are not really defined and are quite random. They come in the form of spots, patches, belts or even combinations of these patterns.

7. Breed standard of the Nigerian dwarf goat

There are a few breeds that have specific guidelines. You can find official clubs dedicated to each of these breeds such as the American Goat Association who have websites that list all necessary characteristics.

Here are the recommended standards for a Nigerian Dwarf Goat:

Head

The head may be long in some cases but it is usually medium sized. The muzzle is generally flat and is dished in rare cases. If the muzzle is dished too sharply, it is usually considered a flaw. Instead, a muzzle that is broad and slightly rounded is always preferred.

As for the jaws, they are well muscled and the lower jaw is full. If the lower jaw is over or under shot, it is considered a flaw in the physical traits.

The eyes of the breed should not protrude too much and must be well placed. They should be apart from one another. The next trait you will look at is the ears. The ears must resemble the regular alpine goat and must always point forward.

Although the horn must face outward, it must never be semi-circular. In the bucks, horns continue to grow for several years. So ideally, at the apex, the horn should continue to grow straight up. The more serious defects in the horn include parallel growth, inward curve and horns that touch each other.

If you feel like the behaviour of an animal might be a threat because of its horns, you may disbud him. If done correctly and neatly, it is still accepted. However, the practice has been widely discouraged.

Neck

The neck must have good muscle mass. In comparison to the Pygmy goats, the dwarf goats have a much more slender neck. It tapers well and is smooth throughout. The neck blends well into the shoulder. Of course, the neck of the females is a lot more slender than that of the bucks. The shoulder blades are set neatly against their body.

Rear Limbs

The rear limbs should have a decent angulation when seen from the side. It should not appear too straight. The legs should be placed moderately apart. They should not appear too cow hocked.

As for the pasterns, they must appear straight, short and strong. The rear limbs must have a decent bone density with good muscling all over.

Rump

The rump should not be too straight or too steep. It is medium in length. The tail must appear symmetrical and must be narrow at the tip. The tail is carried over the back.

The hips must reveal the dairy character of this breed. The pin bones are present lower than the hip and are quite wide and pronounced. The thurls of the goat are placed wide apart. There should be prominent muscling all over.

Feet

The feet must be proportional to the size of the goat. It must be well shaped, even and strong. The hooves also need to be completely symmetrical and should have decent heel depth.

The Skin and Hair

The skin of the goat should be clear and resilient. The coat must be shiny. Remember, you can determine the health of your animal from the appearance of the skin and coat.

The Mammary System

The udder is quite large in size. It should not be pendulous. The texture of the udder must be smooth and firm without any scar tissue or lumps. The attachment at the rear should be high and symmetrical. In the front, it must blend into the body without any pockets.

Buck Reproductive System

The testicles should be equal in size and must be firm. There are two teats that are non-functional in the males.

These are the standard characteristics that you must look out for when you are choosing a Nigerian Dwarf Goat.

8. Why choose miniature livestock?

They are extremely docile creatures and are quite entertaining when they are in a herd. They will interact with you, head butt you when you don't pay attention and even follow you around if they are fond of you. The kids are extremely adorable. Watching them progress from simply stumbling to prancing around your yard is the best thing you can experience.

As for the commercial side to having goats, you can benefit a lot from breeding goats if you know how to do it right. If you have a rare breed that you want to breed and multiply in numbers, you can learn the art or seek assistance from professionals.

The next thing is showing your goats. There are several pet shows that have a special category for farm animals like goats. If you are interested in exhibiting your pet, you will have a lot to do from the word go. You need to groom and take very good care of your goat.

The best thing about miniature livestock is that they have the same qualities as their large sized counterparts. They are also more convenient to manage in an urban set up. That is why several farm owners are switching to miniature livestock. Some of the best reasons to own miniature livestock are:

They don't need much space

In the case of full sized livestock, you need five acres for two heads. In case of miniature livestock you can have two per acre of land. This depends on the grass available and the supplements that you provide with the feed.

Livestock do well when raised in herds. It is possible to have one or more herds even on a smaller property when you raise miniature livestock.

Milk

Of course, on a larger scale, goat's milk is a good business venture. However that requires a good deal of investment. In any case, you can have access to fresh goat milk for your entire family, for sure.

Of course, not everyone needs to be an expert at goat keeping. But, you need to be prepared with all the information that you need. This book covers all the subjects including how to choose a suitable breed, how to take care of the goat, how to feed them and even how to ensure that they are always healthy. If you are a first time goat owner, this is the perfect book for you.

Gentler personality

In comparison to their large sized counterparts, miniature livestock tend to be more docile. Since they are small in size and easy to manage, their owners work directly with them from birth. That makes it possible to halter train them at a very young age. It is also much easier to control miniature livestock should they get out of hand.

The fact that they are easier to handle makes them a better choice for women and also to those who have retired. With large livestock, it can be a little intimidating, especially if you have kids at home.

Return on investment

Miniature livestock can be pricey. In order to get started, you will have to make a big investment. It depends on the rarity of the breed, the availability and the breeding heritage.

In some cases, breeds that have been developed with specific traits and qualities can cost tens of thousands of dollars. But, when you enter your livestock into breeding programs, you may be able to create more than one specimen of your breed or may be lucky enough to develop new species altogether. Either way, you will be able to get guaranteed returns on your investments with miniature livestock.

Varied uses

One of the most important reasons for the increased popularity of smaller livestock is their value on farms and in commercial purposes. They have in fact proved to be a lot more efficient in terms of pork production, breeding and also as show livestock.

Of course, they also make great pets besides being very useful commercially. They have a very friendly nature that also makes them perfect for petting zoos and to educate more people through agro-tourism.

Selling miniature livestock or using them for the same can be good business. The population of miniatures is still low in comparison to the regular sized ones but the demand increases by almost 20% per annum.

There are requirements that include a good record about the heritage of the livestock, documentation of their size when they are born, the immunization records and also the ease of calving. You can sell the breeding samples of your miniature livestock for a good price. Per straw of breeding sample can earn you between $50-100/£10-50. You can sell embryos of as high as $1500/£700.

Of course meat production is an important use. Today healthy and hormone free meat is in demand and that makes miniature livestock a good option for farm owners. Meat production is, of course, one of the biggest income generators for farm owners. There are certain breeds that provide both and have, therefore, become popular.

You do not have to worry about quantity either. With breeds like Nigerian dwarf goats, you don't have to compromise on the butterfat content and the protein content. If you are raising miniature livestock as pets, this can become a source of meat for your family.

Miniature breeds are eligible for several national and state level livestock shows which have attractive cash prizes. The sheer interest in miniature livestock and the curiosity about them has become a USP, promoting their use in livestock shows. The respective clubs for miniature livestock have also started special shows in various categories such as pre-junior categories for younger kids and goats.

Of course, they are increasingly becoming popular as house pets. While this is still a new practice, several farms and breeders have reported an increase in sales solely to keep miniature livestock as pets. Keeping a Nigerian dwarf goat as a pet comes with several benefits. Aside from the fact that they make great companions, they are also great lawn mowers and produce a good amount of manure.

There are a few concerns with miniature livestock making their way into the urban set up. One of them is space. You need to have ample space for the livestock to graze. Fenced areas with adequate housing is very important. You also need to have good back up when you need to travel. It is, after all, not as simple as getting your neighbor or friend to take care of your pet dog or cat.

We will deal with these concerns in the following chapters. The thing with Nigerian dwarf goats is that they are cheaper than their full sized counterparts but do require good funding in order to raise healthy pets. Only when you are prepared to take good care of them and have the resources to do so should you buy miniature livestock for your home.

Once you have a Nigerian dwarf goat or billy, they can perform small tasks like drawing carts and mowing your lawn. Of course, they make very loving and gentle pets.

9. Things to know before you buy the Nigerian dwarf goat

It is better that you plan the costs that you will incur while raising the Nigerian dwarf goat well in advance. This planning will help you to avoid any kind of disappointment that you might face when there are some payments that need to be made. It is better if you plan these costs well in advance, so that you don't get in a fix at the later stage.

There are basically two kinds of costs that you will be looking to incur, which are as follows:

The one-time or initial costs: The initial costs are the costs that you will have to bear in the very beginning of the process of domestication of the animal. This will include the one-time payment that you will give to buy the animal.

There are other costs that would come under this category. The initial costs that you will face when you have decided to domesticate a Nigerian dwarf goat are the purchasing cost of the animal, the permits and the license cost, the vaccines, costs of food containers and the costs of the enclosure.

The regular or monthly costs: Even when you are done with the one-time payments, there are some other costs that you won't be able to avoid. But, these costs can be planned well in advance. You can maintain a journal to keep track of these costs.

The monthly costs are the costs that you will have to spend each month or once in few months to raise the Nigerian dwarf goat. The costs will include the costs of the food requirements and health requirements of the pet.

The various regular veterinarian visits, the sudden veterinarian visits and replacement of things come under the monthly costs category.

The various costs you can expect

While you are all excited to domesticate the Nigerian dwarf goat, you should also start planning for the costs that you will incur. You can expect to incur the following the costs:

Cost of buying the Nigerian dwarf goat

If you are planning to buy a Nigerian dwarf goat from a pet shop, then you can expect to pay somewhere around $750/ £536 to $3000/ £2144. But, this is only the buying cost of the Nigerian dwarf goat; you will have to pay for the vaccinations of the animal also. These vaccinations could cost you around $750/ £286.

You should make sure that you get the Nigerian dwarf goat medically tested before buying it. The examination and tests will also add on to the initial cost. You also have the option to adopt a Nigerian dwarf goat. This will help you to avoid the initial buying cost, though the other costs for raising the Nigerian dwarf goat will remain essentially the same.

Cost of shelter

When you bring a pet home, you have to make the necessary arrangements to give it a comfortable home. The shelter of the animal will be his home, so it is important that you construct the shelter according to the animal's needs.

This is a one-time cost, so you should not try to save money at the cost of the pet's comfort. The cost of shelter will depend on the type of the shelter. You can expect to spend anywhere between $300/ £215 to $400/ £286 for the shelter of the Nigerian dwarf goat.

Cost of food

This is important because if the animal does not get all the appropriate nutrients in the right amount, his health will suffer, which again will be an extra cost for you. So, make sure that you provide all the necessary nutrients to your pet animal.

You should be prepared to spend about $300/ £215 on the diet of your pet every month. The costs will vary depending on various factors, such as the brand of products that you choose and also your exact location.

Cost of health care

It is important to invest in the health of a pet animal. This is necessary because an unhealthy animal is the breeding ground of many other diseases in the home. Your pet might pass on the diseases to other pets if not treated on time. This means danger for the pets and also the members of the family.

You will have to take the Nigerian dwarf goat to the veterinarian for regular visits on his health. He will be able to guide you regarding any medications and vaccines that the pet may need.

It is advised that for the very first year of domestication, you are extra careful regarding the health of the animal. You should be prepared to spend $300/ £215 to $400/ £286.

Other costs

Although the main costs that you will encounter while raising your pet have already been discussed, there will be some extra costs that you will have to take care of. Most of these costs are one-time costs.

You will have to spend money to buy stuff such as Nigerian dwarf goat bedding, accessories, food and water bowls and toys for the pet.

You can expect to spend some $300/ £215 on these costs. The cost will depend on the wear and tear and the quality of the products. In order to keep a track of the costs that could be awaiting you, you should regularly check the various items in the cage of the pet.

10. Bringing home a healthy Nigerian dwarf goat

The following pointers will help you to make sure that your future pet is in the prime of its health:

- Even if the animal has had health issues in the past, it can be a matter of concern for you.

- If you are buying an older Nigerian dwarf goat, you need to be all the more vigilant because they could carry some infections.

- All good breeders will maintain a health card, which will have all the details of past diseases and infections. This health card will also help you to understand the vaccine cycle of the animal.

- It is important that you closely examine your prospective pet. You should look for any abrasions on his skin.

- His skin should not be torn or bruised.

- Never accept previous blood tests or the ones provided to you by the breeder. You must invest in a complete test yourself before the dwarf is delivered.

- You must not accept a delivery at short notice. You must have everything in place on your property for your new pet.

- Do not buy any livestock that is being sold in a hurry.

- Don't rush into a purchase. Plan well and investigate the breeding facility well.

- You should make it a point to check the body temperature of the Nigerian dwarf goat. The body temperature should be normal.

- You should closely look for any kind of injuries. If you find anything that does not seem normal, then you need to discuss it with the breeder.

- The Nigerian dwarf goat should not have any broken limbs. You should be able to check this manually.

- You should discuss at length about the concerns that you have regarding the Nigerian dwarf goat.

- You should follow all the instructions that the vet gives you because they will be for the benefit of the animal.

- You should only keep the Nigerian dwarf goat if you are convinced that you will be able to care for the little animal.

Chapter 2: Owning a Nigerian dwarf goat

If you wish to own a Nigerian dwarf goat or even if you already own one, it is important to understand the basic characteristics of the animal. You should know what you can expect from the animal and what you can't.

As for goats, they are seldom found in the urban set up. They are usually raised in large numbers on farms and also in designated commercial set ups where there is ample professional help available to take care of these animals.

If you are planning to bring a goat home, on the other hand, you must invest a lot more time doing your homework and research about this animal in the first place. You must be sure that you can take on this responsibility before you make a commitment.

You see, the goat is a large animal. This means that you need to have enough space in your home to begin with. It is definitely not possible, and even unethical to cram a goat up in a tiny apartment. They need exercise and a lot of space in order to remain healthy.

You may choose to keep your goat in your backyard or even in a designated space outdoors. Once you do that, you need to worry about keeping them fenced and protected. If you are keeping a goat in an urban set up, the last thing you want is your pet goat breaking free and running out into the freeway.

When you bring a goat home, you must be prepared to let it stay true to its instincts. If you find a goat cute, it is alright. However, if you expect your goat to cuddle up and sleep in the same bed with you, it is time for you to consider other options for a pet.

Your goat will not fetch the morning newspaper or sit on the couch while you watch TV either. It is an outdoor pet. This is a very important thing you need to tell yourself several times before you bring home a goat.

Now, if you are willing to let the goat be a goat, you need to progress onto the next step. The kind of food and the care that your goat needs is pretty different from the conventional pet. They have specific requirements that help them stay healthy. We will discuss that in more detail. However, what you must understand is that clean drinking water and the right kind of food is extremely essential for your goat's health.

There are a few considerations that you need to make before you bring a Nigerian dwarf goat home:

- You need to have a large enough space for each member of your herd.
- You must have enough finances to provide good quality food and healthcare for your pets.
- They need to have a place to take shelter and rest.
- You need to be aware of the right way to interact with your Nigerian dwarf goats to stay safe and to make sure that the animals are not stressed.

There are a few things that you have to keep prepared before you bring your Nigerian dwarf goat home.

1. Where to buy a Nigerian dwarf goat

There first step is to figure out the best source for your Nigerian dwarf goat. The most common options include:

- A breeder: There are commercial and hobby breeders who work towards producing a single breed of dwarf livestock or try to experiment with different breeds and genetic lines. You need to make sure that the breeder that you are planning to buy from has positive testimonies, maintains a clean and hygienic environment for his goats and kids and has ample knowledge about dwarfs.

- A primary owner: Sometimes, owners may be interested in selling or giving away kids that were born in their yard or farm. These individuals are not breeders and are probably the best source as they do not have any agenda with their kids. These people are genuinely concerned about the health and safety of the herd.

- Auctions: in the case of rare breeds, there may be auctions at state shows and fairs. This is risky as you do not know what health or behavioral issues the goat or billy may have. Buying from an auction is generally not recommended for first time buyers.

- Rescue/shelter: This is the most economical option available to you. However, the breed may be poor in quality and may come with several health issues as well.

-

Buying options with dwarf goats

When you buy your Nigerian dwarf goat, make sure that you choose the breed according to the purpose that it will serve on your farm. We have discussed the qualities of different breeds in the previous chapter. Since they are extremely expensive, learning all you can about your preferred breed will help you choose a healthy specimen.

Always make sure that you buy from reputable breeder. Secondly, you must insist on a health check up by a vet before you bring one home.

If you want to get started with your miniature herd right away, you can choose purebred adults and breeding stock. They are the most expensive option and are also not easily available in most cases. You can consider buying kids because they are more readily available.

The disadvantage with kids is that they do not come with a breeding guarantee. So if the billy grows up to be poor in production, you will lose out on your investment. A billy is a good option if you are not particularly interested in breeding and are looking for a low price option.

For some breeds, it is also possible to purchase the embryos. But you can do so only if you have the knowledge and facilities or necessary assistance for successful embryo transfers in your livestock.

You have the option of buying frozen embryos or one that has been implanted in a female already. The latter is the cheaper and safer option. In case of embryo implantation, the success rate varies. It is usually about 60% on average.

In case you decide to purchase frozen embryos, you must consider meeting a reproductive specialist who deals with livestock solely. Make sure you gain as much knowledge as possible. It is also important to choose a healthy goat for implantation.

There are many risks with purchasing embryos. The success rate is not 100% to begin with. You also cannot determine the gender of the billy that will be born. Only when you are looking for an extremely rare breed, you may not have too many other options to pursue.

Adopting a Nigerian dwarf goat

Some farms will put their kids up for adoption. You may also adopt one from a rescue shelter. In case of the latter option, be prepared for possible behavioral issues in the goat as they may have had a history of abuse or poor treatment.

Now, with adoption, you only have to pay an adoption fee for your goat or billy. This starts as low as $30 or £12 depending upon the medical history of the animal and the expenses borne for the animal.

The goats, or kids, up for adoption will be listed on the website of the shelter or farm that you plan to adopt from. You can look for one with all the desirable traits. Make sure that you visit the animal that you have chosen at least once to ensure that the temperament suits your home. You need to be particularly careful when you are adopting a billy as you need to be cautious when you are approaching them, especially when the breeding season is on.

Once you have transferred the adoption fee, you will have to send in all your personal details. They may require a few documents of identity as well. Then, the miniature livestock that you have selected will either be delivered to your home or you may have to pick him up, depending upon the conditions of the place you are adopting from.

Some of them insist on house checks as well. Once the adoption process is complete, it is good to get your pet checked by a vet immediately. In some cases, you will be able to get a health guarantee that allows you to return the animal you adopted, provided he has been checked in less than 72 hours of delivery.

Choosing the best breed

Once you have found a good breeder whom you can buy a good miniature livestock breed from, the next step is to decide which one suits you best. Each breed has a different requirement and temperament that you need to cater to.

The origin of the breed is the first thing that you must consider. The next thing is to understand the breeds that your dwarf is a mixture of. This will help broadly determine the characteristics of the breed and the type of environment that you will need to provide.

Your interest in bringing home a Nigerian dwarf goat is also important. The resources available and the type of care that you will be able to provide will also determine which breed you must choose as a pet.

If you are looking for a herd, you need to consider factors like the local climate, the weather pattern, the type of pasture that you have and the space available. Some breeds are adaptable to cold climates, specifically the double coated ones, and others will do well in hot climates.

Try to learn as much as you can about the breed that you have set your mind on. The more you learn, the more you will be able to look into the details of their behavior. For example, Angus livestock are known for their marbling ability while Herefords are known for being placid in nature and also for their high feed efficiency.

If it costs more to feed them, you may not have too much profit. It is best that you find a hardier breed that will be able to function even with marginal pastures if you are looking at a commercial venture. If they are good at calving, you will also see that the goat will stay longer with the herd, providing more milk.

In the end, the only thing that determines what breed that you choose is the purpose of bringing one home. Some are specifically chosen as companions, some make great show animals and some are commercially more viable.

It is recommended that you choose local breeds as they are likely to adapt faster. They will be able to handle the weather fluctuations and will be healthier. However, with the right resources, you can raise a healthy herd of any breed.

As long as you are willing to learn more and provide for your pet, you can choose any breed for your home. But, do not make a choice because you have a favorite when you also know that it will be a challenge to provide for him or her.

2. Advantages and disadvantages of domesticating Nigerian dwarf goats

If you have already bought or adopted a Nigerian dwarf goat, this section will help you. The list of pros and cons of Nigerian dwarf goats will help you to prepare yourself for the challenges that lie ahead of you. This list will help you to be a better parent to the pet and to form an ever-lasting bond with your beloved pet.

Advantages of domesticating a Nigerian dwarf goat:

If you are still not sure about adopting or buying a Nigerian dwarf goat, then you should know that there are many pros of domesticating a Nigerian dwarf goat. They are loved by their owners and their families because of some amazing qualities that they possess.

This animal can definitely prove to be a great pet for your household and your family.

The various advantages of domesticating a Nigerian dwarf goat are as follows:

- The size of the Nigerian dwarf goat makes it an ideal choice as a pet.

- Their looks make them adorable and cute to look at. They are loved by one and all. Who wouldn't want to have a pet that it beautiful to look at?

- People who love pets that can be lifted and cuddled will love the Nigerian dwarf goat. A Nigerian dwarf goat will allow you to lift it and play with it.

- This pet will be the centre of affection for all the family members and also for each and every visitor of the house.

- Nigerian dwarf goats are known to be very loyal animals. They will love your presence around them and will show you that they love you by their own unique ways.

- If they establish a trust factor with you, they will always remain loyal to you. Loyalty is a very good trait in an animal. This is a great quality to have in a domesticated animal.

- Nigerian dwarf goats are also known to possess great intelligence. You should be prepared to witness their intelligent antics and gimmicks. They will actually surprise you with their intelligence.

- A Nigerian dwarf goat is a very sharp animal. It is always good to have a pet that is intelligent and sharp.

- If you care well for the pet, he will also respond in a very positive way. When the Nigerian dwarf goat is in a happy mood, he will jump around the entire space. His unique ways and antics will leave you in splits.

- They are very entertaining. If you just sit around a Nigerian dwarf goat, you are bound to have a great time.

- If there are kids in your home, then they will fall in love with this pet. But, you should monitor the interaction of the kids with the pet. This is important to keep everyone safe and sound.

- The Nigerian dwarf goats don't overeat, so you don't have to worry in this aspect. You can leave food in the container and the Nigerian dwarf goat will eat as much as is required. They are used to eating several small meals.

- The Nigerian dwarf goats can be trained. You can teach them some easy tricks to have more fun with them.

- A very important point to note here is that their demeanour will depend a lot on how they are raised. The preparation has to begin right from the start. You can't expect them to suddenly become friendly after years of wrong treatment. If they are raised to be social, they will be very social.

- Nigerian dwarf goats live in groups in their natural environment. This makes them tolerant towards other Nigerian dwarf goats. The Nigerian dwarf goats will wrestle and play with each other. There is a very slight possibility that they will not get along.

- Nigerian dwarf goats have a fairly long life, if they are taken care of. You can make a strong emotional bond with your pet and can enjoy the fruits of the bond for years to come.

Disadvantages of domesticating a Nigerian dwarf goat:

The adorable and friendly animal has his own set of challenges when it comes to domesticating them. It is important to understand these disadvantages so that you can be better prepared for them. Following are the disadvantages of raising a Nigerian dwarf goat:

- Miniature livestock can be pricey. In order to get started, you will have to make a big investment.

- Nigerian dwarf goats are considered very high maintenance. You should be ready to spend money and time on these pets.

- The eyesight of goats is very poor. They are almost blind. This can be a real challenge for most owners. They indulge in rooting habits to locate food. This can be very messy. You can expect large amounts of mess in your home.

- Though the animal is miniature, you can expect it to attain a weight of over 50 pounds. This can be a problem for many. If you are looking for an animal that is less in weight, then you will be disappointed.

- They are definitely not suitable for someone who is looking for a quiet and calm pet. They are energetic, will run around and will also make noises.

- Because of his energy levels, the Nigerian dwarf goat can run into things and can get hurt very easily.

- The animal seeks a lot of attention. The Nigerian dwarf goat is a kind of pet that will require you to pamper him a lot.

- The pet can get stressed and depressed if he is left lonely for longer durations. You can't leave him in the cage for too long.

- The cost that you will incur while buying and raising is more when compared to other pets, such as the dog and the cat.

- The pet has a very inactive lifestyle. This can lead to many health issues.

- The pet is prone to stress. This can also lead to many diseases and health related issues in the pet animal.

3. Transport and handling

Once you have decided the breed of miniature livestock that you want to bring home, you can look for a reliable source. The next thing that you should do is to make sure that you transport your livestock in the right way to reduce any stress that is related to travelling.

There are legal considerations when you transport livestock to make it a more humane process. According to the Code of Accepted Farm Practice for the Welfare of Livestock, here are a few things that you need to keep in mind when you are brining your pet home:

The transport vehicle should be of the appropriate size and design to make sure that your entire stock can be transported comfortably.

The transport vehicle should be in good condition. That way, you will not have any injuries due to protrusions or other issues in the container. You can also ensure that the livestock will reach the destination on time without any delay due to breakdowns.

The stock crate should be examined thoroughly. It should be smooth and the contact surface should not have any protrusions.

In case the transport crate has any pens, they should not be more than 3 meters in length. That way the animals will have enough support during the travel and will also feel less stressed as a result of that.

It is best that you hire a trailer or a transport truck for your dwarf livestock. The front of the trailer should be solid enough to protect the billy from any wind. The animal that is being transported should be checked on at least every 3 hours.

You must feed the animal 6 hours before you transport him or her. The number of animals in the trailer should be such that they can lie down when they are being transported.

Never transport a dwarf goat or billy in the boot of your car or in a sealed container that does not allow air flow. The legs of the animals must never be tied to restrain them.

The trailer should never be overloaded. Even if it means that you may have to make multiple trips, the trailer should only have as many as it can accommodate comfortably.

These simple precautions will ensure that your Nigerian dwarf goat does not feel very stressed after the journey. That way, it will be easy for you to introduce the animal into your property on the first day.

4. Introducing your new livestock to an existing herd

If you already have a small herd, miniature livestock or regular sized livestock, proper introduction is the key to maintaining peace within the herd. What you can be sure of is that there will not be any ugly fights.

They tend to establish the pecking order quite peacefully. But, with introduction of new livestock, the biggest concern is potential health risks to the existing herd.

You need to make sure that all precautions are taken before you allow your new pet to graze with the existing herd or even stay with them in the same housing area.

Precautions to avoid diseases

Even when you have the healthiest Nigerian dwarf goat added to the property, you must remember that the immunity of the animal will be compromised because of the transport stress, the new environment and the change in food and water. This is one of the main reasons why you need to take all the precautions possible before you introduce the animal to the existing herd.

Even before you transport the new goat, you need to have a complete blood test done. Look for an authorized lab or consult your vet before you agree to buy a dwarf.

It is advisable to keep your new goat quarantined in a separate enclosure for a minimum of 14 days. It is better if you can quarantine for 60 days. This will give the new animal ample time to get accustomed to the new place and will also give you a chance to observe closely for any signs of disease.

Introduction to the herd

For the most part, your dwarf will be safe in a herd when introduced. Livestock seldom get into aggressive fights. But, if you have regular sized goats and kids in your herd, taking precaution is necessary. The sheer size of the other animals can lead to dominant behavior.

A temporary fence can be placed between the new pet and the existing herd when you let them all out to graze. Supervise the herd during this period to see how they respond. If they are not very alert and practically ignore the newcomer, it is a good sign. You can keep them in adjacent pastures for a few days to help them get used to the smell and sight of one another. This is recommended especially if you are introducing a billy to a herd which already has a mature billy.

It is a good idea to avoid any introduction of a new billy during the mating season. This can lead to some squabble. When you let the new member interact with the herd without a fence, it should be monitored at all times initially. If there is any sign of head butting or chasing, you must isolate the new goat or billy immediately.

When you feel like the herd is getting along with the new member, allow short unsupervised introductions. Leave them together for half an hour and come back to check on them. This time period can increase slowly as they get used to each other.

It is advisable to separate polled and horned animals. If possible, you can have a separate herd of Nigerian dwarf goats and one with regular sized goats. That way, there is no room for dominant behavior at any point.

If you do notice any bruises or cuts, contact your vet to understand the source. This also brings us to an important point of introducing the new member to the herd on a weekday. That way, you can be sure that the vet is available in case there is any untoward incident or injury to the new animal.

5. Introducing a dwarf to other animals

If you have a pet dog at home, it is necessary to make the introduction correctly. With pets like cats, the risk is lower as they will not approach the goat or billy in most cases. The interactions are also limited because of the nature of cats. That said, even cats must not be left unsupervised with your goats. The size difference means that the cat is at the risk of being kicked or trampled if he startles the goat.

But, with dogs, they usually run around in the yard and will frequently interact with your new Nigerian dwarf goat. So, proper introductions are necessary.

The first introduction should be with your dog on a leash. Watch the dog's reaction. Frothing at the mouth, the tail pointing upwards or a hunting position means that your dog is in an attack mode. This is natural the first time they meet. If you can calm your dog down and let him watch the goats while on leash, do so. If not, try to introduce them again.

With frequent meetings, the dogs will become less responsive in an aggressive manner. It is still not safe to let the dog run freely around the goat. To begin with, the dog has a natural predatory instinct towards a goat. Second, a startled goat can cause serious damage to a dog with one single blow with his strong legs.

Allow them to interact with a temporary fence in between. Keep an eye on your dog's reaction. With regular and controlled meetings, the dog will begin to ignore the goat and lose interest in her completely.

Only a dog who is obedience trained is safe to leave with the goats without any barrier. The most important commands that your dog must respond to are stay and come. If you do not get your dog to respond every time, work on his obedience skills before he is let out with the goats.

Some livestock owners and farm owners suggest an e-collar to prevent any attacks. However, the safer way and the gentler option is to train your dog to obey commands flawlessly. This is one of the most important things for dogs that will work on farms. Once they are trained and comfortable, you can even get your dog to herd livestock for you and keep them from escaping from your farm or yard.

Special training is available for herding dogs. You can look for trainers who will help you with this and make your dog an important part of your journey with your Nigerian dwarf goat.

If you are lucky, the first interaction itself will be calm and easy. If not, work with your dog and help him make new friends.

Chapter 3: Decoding the Nigerian dwarf goat's behaviour

A Nigerian dwarf goat is a small, naughty animal that will keep you busy and entertained by all its unique antics and mischiefs. It is said that each animal is different from the other. Each one will have some traits that are unique to him.

While you will learn about all the unique traits that your particular Nigerian dwarf goat has by experiencing him and spending time with him, there are some traits that almost all Nigerian dwarf goats will exhibit. It is beneficial to know of these traits so that you are not taken off guard. You will be able to understand what is normal for this animal and what is not.

There is no doubt that Nigerian dwarf goats make great pets. They are affectionate and are also extremely friendly. You can find a great companion in your Nigerian dwarf goat provided you spend some time to understand their behavior and make a connection.

Nigerian dwarf goats are known to be great show animals. This means that they can also be trained with ease with some commitment. This section explains the general behavior of goats and kids to help you understand how to have more positive interactions with your pet and also stay safe when doing so.

1. Understanding the behavior of your Nigerian dwarf goat

In the case of miniature livestock, you need be aware of all the senses that they use. There is more to livestock than just vision. This is the key to proper interaction without startling the animal.

Goats are capricious creatures. This means that they are extremely whimsical and quite comical at times. However, you must never underestimate the capacities of your goats. They are curious creatures and are extremely intelligent.

Goats are often considered to be very aloof and unloving. But this, in my opinion, is the biggest myth as far as goats are concerned. They are really lovely creatures who love to play and be around people.

However, you need to understand that your goat is nothing like the dog you have at home. Unlike dogs, goats are not looking for your approval. They will be attached to you, no doubt, but they are going to behave just like any other goat and not worry about you being pleased with them.

So, if you are expecting your goat to jump up onto your lap, I would hate to bust your fairytale expectations. Nevertheless, goats are wonderful pets and give you several opportunities to interact with them and play with them. However, for them to get comfortable around you, you need to be able to understand their behavior. That is when you can create a sense of trust between you and your goat.

What you need to understand also is that the behavior of goats changes rather drastically from the time when they are kids to the time that they become mature. The only way you can familiarize yourself with goat behavior is by spending enough time with your goats. That way, you will also be able to understand herd behavior along with individual goat behavior properly.

2. Reading the dwarf's mannerisms

Even in some of the most well established farms, people are seldom aware of the right way to approach livestock. This results in animals that are extremely stressed and uncomfortable. It affects their productivity and in the worst cases can provoke an attack from the animal.

Reading the body language of your pet can really help you create that special bond that you dream of. For instance, if a goat is relaxed, he will stretch after standing up. If he is under any kind of stress, the common behavior includes bellowing, butting and even kicking. These behaviors are clear indicators that the immediate environment needs to be changed.

Hiding or getting lost

This is something that goat kids are great at. They usually get into little holes and spaces where they can hide. Then, they sit there really quietly. This is a natural instinct that helps them survive in a herd. If there are any spaces on your property that could act as caves, you will most often find them hiding in these caves.

If you thought that the mother would be able to find her kids, you are seriously mistaken. Several studies over the years have found that kids are so good at hiding that even the moms can't find them. Most often, the mother would just wander away with no clue of where the kid is.

Several goat owners that I know have told me that they have been unable to locate kids for hours and sometimes overnight. Then they are found in the herd the next day or under a pile of things in a secluded corner.

To be prepared for this devious hiding, you may want to use brightly coloured collars that will help you locate them easily.

Chewing

Undoubtedly, baby goats love to explore. Just like the babies of other species of animals, baby goats, too, love to explore with their mouths. So, they will chew on things and ruin them a little to learn more about them.

Climbing

Baby goats love to climb. In fact, they love to climb on their moms. This is allowed only with the mom and not with any other herd member. Essentially, a baby goat will climb only on members of the family.

So, if you see a little kid trying to climb you, then, you should feel really privileged. Climbing is a baby goat's way of having a good time. They actually consider anything that they can climb as toys. This includes a fallen tree, logs, spools of cable, a picnic table and play forts that you can build for them.

Sneezing

This is a behaviour pattern that they will carry on into their adulthood. In goats, sneezing is not a sign of illness. It is actually a warning sign. If you see your goat sneezing, you must know that there is some danger (like a predator) lurking around. If the sneeze is not too tensed or alarmed, it could just be a part of a game.

Head Butting

Head butting among kids is quite different from head butting among adults. It is less aggressive and is usually playful. It is a good idea to help the kids practice head butting. If you gently push the head of a kid, he will push back. However, you must remember never to push the forehead. This is important especially if the goats are a little big. It may lead to an aggressive reaction that could be dangerous for you. When you push the forehead of a goat, you are threatening his position in the herd.

3. Behavior of the adult goat

Among adult goats, all their behaviour patterns are directed towards maintaining their position in a herd. Yes, they can be playful at times. However, the main agenda is to show their worth in a herd.

Another significant behaviour change or pattern is when your goat is trying to send out signs that he is ready for mating or when she is nursing. Here are some common behaviour patterns you can observe in adult goats:

Fighting and dominance

The herd dynamics in goats is ever changing. Every goat has the ability to attain the position of the top buck or the flock queen if he or she can fight it out. So, you will see fighting quite commonly among adult goats.

Fighting is pronounced when new goats are introduced into a herd. If you do not find any animal in danger, there is no need to intervene as this is natural for goats.

If a doe has kidded recently or if she is about to kid, she will try to improve her status in the herd. This is primarily an attempt to get her kids a better status. During these times, you cannot do much but let them fight it out even if it is too aggressive.

Goats also take sides when there is a fight. They tend to become helpers to the two goats who are in the main fight. The fights include several signs of aggression such as:

Pawing

When a doe has just given birth to kids, she engages in pawing. This is her way of getting the kids to stand up and start moving around. If you think that she is attacking the kids, let me tell you that this is her way of showing that she cares.

However, you need to watch the pawing closely if you notice that the mother is very enthusiastic. In some cases, she may kill the kid accidentally.

This is not a sign of refusal either. When a mother refuses her new born, she will butt it or just ignore it.

Sexual behaviour

Both does and bucks show similar reactions when they are in heat. Here are some signs that will tell you that your goat is in heat:

Tongue flapping: The buck will flap his tongue on the sides of the doe he is interested in. A buck may also initiate this behaviour or reciprocate this way.

Leg pawing: Along with the tongue flapping the buck will also straighten his leg and paw the sides of the doe.

Urinating

Urinating is a sign of when the bucks go into heat or into a rut. You will notice that they spray on their front legs and on their faeces. Bucks actually have a special attachment on the genitalia to do this. He will even spray it into the mouth, curl up the lips and smell it. He does this to coat himself with his sticky urine that the does find attractive. Cologne for goats, I guess.

Developing an odour

You will notice that bucks begin to smell really bad as they grow. For some this smell is not exactly bad but is rather strong. The odour becomes worse with maturity. If you are interested in milking the does, keep them away from such bucks as the smell could creep into the milk.

Goats exhibit several other distinct herd and individual habits that you will need to get used to. You will become familiar with these habits as you observe your goats and interact with them.

Chapter 4: Setting up the Nigerian dwarf goat's home

Like you need a home, an animal also needs a place and space that he can call his home. A home should make him happy and should be inviting for him. When the home does not provide the comfort and security that it should, it can lead to detrimental results.

There are many owners who might feel that there is no need to set up a cage because the pet can stay indoors. But, you need to remember that even if you are a hands-on parent of the pet, there will be times when the pet would be unsupervised.

The cage should be built keeping in mind the basic nature of the Nigerian dwarf goat. You can't build a cage that is suitable for a tiger or a bird. You have a Nigerian dwarf goat and your cage should be built keeping in mind his natural behaviour, instincts, likes and dislikes. This is the best for you and also for the Nigerian dwarf goat.

You should understand that just because the Nigerian dwarf goat is a small animal does not mean that you can keep it anywhere. You need a proper cage for him. You should never keep him in a glass environment such as an aquarium. Such places don't allow the flow of air and can cause breathing issues in the Nigerian dwarf goat.

It is important to have the right temperature for the Nigerian dwarf goat. If the temperature is more than eighty degrees Fahrenheit or less than forty five degrees Fahrenheit, it is advised to keep the pet inside the house in controlled temperatures. Nothing is more important than the health and well-being of the pet.

There are different ways of keeping a herd. You can either have an extensive area for grazing or can keep the herd in a closed confinement. But, it is your responsibility to make sure that you provide for the welfare of your herd. In fact not providing ample shelter from extreme weather conditions will lead to animal cruelty in many states.

A healthy herd can tolerate weather changes to a large extent provided they have good access to fresh water and food and have been acclimatized. In any case, providing shelter will ensure that no production ability is lost. When the herd does not have enough shelter, a lot of their energy goes into just taking care of normal functions.

If the temperature goes above or below the average temperature that the animal can handle, you have to make sure that you provide them with adequate shelter. It is possible for deaths to occur in your herd because of extreme weather conditions.

1. The best shelter options

The shelter that you provide must be able to protect the animals from cold breezes. Some of the best options are:

- Shelters with wind breaks. You will see that the livestock will rub up against the wind break to stay warm. So, you need to make sure that the wind break is strong and safe.

- If you have a shelterbelt of trees, it will be able to keep the livestock safe from winds. There is a shelter zone that is usually up to about 14 times the height of the shelterbelt.

- Make sure that there are trees in the north-south direction as most wind flow will be in the north and south western direction.

- Paddocks and gullies make for good shelter against cold.

When you plant a shelter belt, make sure that the trees are spaced out evenly. That ensures wind flow without too much turbulence.

You must not allow any pregnant livestock to graze in paddocks that have Yellow or Monterey pine trees. If the fallen branches and twigs are ingested, it poses a great threat to the fetus.

You can build one sided sheds for your livestock. Temporary shelter can be built using plastic tarpaulins and shade cloth if you do not have any other shelter option.

Shelter is one of the most important parts of proper husbandry of miniature livestock.

2. Building housing areas

Shelterbelts cannot be created overnight. It may take several months for the shelterbelt to grow properly. In case you do not have trees to protect your miniature livestock during adverse weather conditions, here are a few housing options that you can try:

- **Single slope, open sided sheds:** This is the most typical housing option. It is suitable for any livestock that you have on your farm. It is easy to build and is also economical. When you build an open sided shelter, make sure that the open end faces south in the winter to block any wind. You also have the option of partitioning the pole barns to make sure that the animals are kept at a distance easily.

- **Clear span open sided shelter:** When you have a clear span, you have ample space to use manure removal equipment. You can open any side of this shelter as per the weather. You have a gable end that should be open when there is any rain or snow. With the gable end open, you have more depth in the bay area, protecting the animal from winds. The back end of this shelter may become damp and will require ventilation and lighting. This is perfect if you have a herd that is smaller than 20 in number.

- **An unused barn:** This structure can be built but it is a better option if you already have one on your farm. You can renovate it as per the requirement of your miniature livestock. This is cheaper than installing a whole new structure. Make sure you have ample access to manure remove. That is why it is recommended that you have a free stall barn instead of a conventional tie stall.

- **Hoop barn:** This is possibly the most expensive type of shelter for your livestock. But it does provide a lot of protection in cold conditions. However, in the warmer months, ventilation can be a problem. If you have ample grazing space for your livestock, this is not really a big concern. A hoop barn looks almost like a green house with a roof that is arched.

Make sure that the design is simple and practical to maintain it well. You must have enough space to make a feed yard to keep the animals comfortable and socialize properly.

The flooring should be covered with some substrate that can absorb waste. The best option is hay. Mud is not a good idea, especially in winter. Evaporation is lower with mud and if the draining is improper, it can become a harbor for several microbes. If the floor is already made of mud, adding bedding like hay can be a good option.

The selected area for housing should be higher than the rest of the land. That will help you get rainwater and waste out easily.

There should be ample light and air supply in the shelter. Sunlight is extremely necessary to keep the shelter dry and prevent any germs or viruses from breeding.

Try to build a shelter in an area that is surrounded by trees. This helps provide additional shade and shelter to the animals.

There should be a good drainage system inside the shelter to make sure that there is no dampness whatsoever. Trash and excreta in the shelter will lead to the growth of viruses, parasites and insects like mosquitos and flies. They transmit diseases that can affect the entire herd in some cases.

The shelter should be covered with some form of fencing. We will discuss the options in the next section.

Make sure that every animal has at least five square meters of space inside the housing area in order to prevent overcrowding and related stress.

It is a good idea to create a separate area of housing to keep any injured or sick animals. This should be a quiet and dry area to prevent any stress.

You must have the shelter ready before you bring your Nigerian dwarf goat home. Make sure that it suits the requirements based on the number of livestock and even the age and gender. Younger livestock and kids will need a shelter that is stronger as they tend to have more energy which means that they are able to apply more force on the walls.

3. Bedding options for Goats

The bedding that you place in their area should be made from a material that will be able to keep the goats warm and dry throughout. It must also be easy to clean.

If the material that you are using has the property of retaining water, then you will notice that it will be very hard to maintain the shelter well. So, for best results, you must use the following bedding options in your shelter:

Pine Shavings

This is the most preferred type of bedding option as goats simply love it. It is ideal for smaller herds. The best thing about pine shavings is that they are highly absorbent. They have the ability to soak in not only the wetness but also the odour of the poop.

They help you manage the litter well. Additionally, pine shavings are also very soft and light. The shavings are extremely easy to replace. They are also highly affordable and easily available. If you are buying pine shavings online, make sure you don't get confused between chips and shavings. Pine chips are terrible bedding options.

Straw and Hay

This is a popular bedding choice among people who have small farms. The reason that it is so popular is that it is extremely affordable and really durable.

It is also a good absorbent that has the ability to soak the wetness and also soak the odor. The quality of the straw and hay is important. If you compromise on this, the straw will remain moist, making the shelter smell really bad.

Shredded Paper

In case you run out of your regular bedding material, shredded paper can make a great alternative. It is also considered one of the most popular trends among livestock owners. This is not only a good bedding option but is also a great way to recycle paper.

The best thing is that you will never run out of it. All you need to do is shred the newspaper in your home into small pieces and lay it on the floor neatly. Newspaper shredding is a great absorbent like any other bedding material. The goats will not be harmed by it at all.

Dirt

Dirt is a really interesting option for shelter bedding. The first and the most important thing is that dirt is completely natural. Hence, it will not harm the animals even a little. Sand, along with the poop can make great compost.

Sawdust

This is a rather novel idea in the world of livestock keeping. Sawdust is great as it is really soft. Sawdust also has a natural smell that keeps the coop fresh all day long. During the colder months, sawdust makes a great bedding option as it can be really warm.

The only disadvantage with sawdust is that it retains water. It is also prone to bacteria. So, you must make sure that you change the sawdust regularly if you choose to use it.

When you are choosing the bedding option for the shelter, there is one more thing that you must consider. If your goats are sharing the space with another pet, you must avoid bedding that will not suit the other animal.

4. Protection from predators

The biggest problem with having goats in your garden is the danger of predators. It is heart-breaking when you realize that one of your beauties has been taken away or killed by a predatory animal. Of course, this is a natural process that you cannot really stop.

What you can do is keep your goats in enclosures when you are not around to supervise, especially at night. You can also build fences to keep the predators away from your herd.

The difficult part is that goats are usually extremely vulnerable when they are domesticated. So, they become easy prey for animals like coyotes and foxes or even bobcats and raccoons. With animals like the coyote, you can even expect attacks in broad daylight. So you must take several preventive measures to ensure that your goats are safe.

Temporary fencing

Temporary fencing serves two purposes. It can be used to separate various farm animals and can also be used to direct them into their enclosures. The primary function of a temporary or portable fence is to mark boundaries and actually control your animal groups.

The most common type of temporary fence is the chain link fence. You can get long rolls of chain links that are arranged in a zigzag pattern. The heavy base allows you to place them where you need. Another simple type of temporary fencing is the mesh fence. It is similar to the chain link fence but is more secure as the base is heavier.

For larger animals like the goat, you can also use a picket fence. They have vertically arranged wires that have a very strong base to keep these animals safe.

If you have poultry in your home, you can use chicken wires or poultry fences to keep goats and chickens separate. These fences are ready to install and can be adjusted as per your needs. They do not require any tools for installation and work perfectly well on all terrains.

Permanent fencing

Permanent fences do not serve the purpose of separating different farm animals. They are used to mark the boundary of your garden to prevent animals from getting out or getting in to your property. For instance, if you have a freeway near your home, a permanent fence will keep your goats from getting away from your garden or farm. They also keep predators at bay.

Needless to say, these structures, once installed, must not be removed. They must also be able to keep small animals and birds from getting in and out. In addition to that, they must also be strong enough to hold on for several years.

The most common type of permanent fencing used to keep your goats safe is wooden or bamboo fencing. Panels of wood and bamboo are installed around the perimeter of your space. You must make sure that there are no gaps in between panels. Concrete fences are also used. They are sturdier and are also great at keeping predators away.

Electric fences are not the best. There are chances that your own pets will get electrocuted. Of course, it is a cruel option whether you are thinking of keeping predators or pets in their boundaries.

5. Best fencing options

Proper fencing is necessary in order to keep your livestock from entering any unsafe area on your property or from walking out onto a busy street. It also ensures that your livestock is safe from any predators.

You also need good fencing to manage grazing. You can control the area that your livestock grazes in so that they only get access to good fodder. This can be done with the help of temporary fencing. Permanent fences are usually used to mark the boundaries of your property.

Whether you are choosing temporary or permanent fencing, here are the options available:

- **Barbed wire fence:** This type of fence consists of several strands of horizontal wire that has barbs every 12cms. Do not use wires that have barbs placed closer as it can lead to injuries.

- **Woven wire fence:** This type of fence contains smooth steel wires that are woven with horizontal and vertical wires. This is one of the most widely used types of fencing. However it is expensive and may not be as useful as high tensile wires.

- **High tensile wires:** You can choose either electric or non-electric fencing. It is more elastic, is lighter and more effective.

- **Interior fencing:** This may include a temporary electric fence or may use a permanent fence that divides the area. This helps livestock stay in one area without any conflict or territorial behavior.

It is common practice to use electric wires. But make sure that your livestock is trained to recognize the electric fence before you introduce them into a pasture with this type of fencing. You can start by using one strand of hot wire at very low voltage near the water sources. Even a mild current is enough for the livestock to recognize an electric fence and make sure that they stay clear of it.

6. Other important equipment

There are a few installations that you must make inside or around the shelter in order to create the perfect ambience for your goats. The three most essential things along with the shelter are:

A sleeping shelf

Goats may sleep indoors or they may just rest outside. This depends entirely upon the weather conditions. However, it is a good idea to have sleeping shelf for your goats to rest.

The most recommended type of sleeping shelf is the triangular one in the corner. These shelves are extremely cosy and are not very space consuming.

You can build a simple sleeping shelf using plywood. It is best that you use pressure treated plywood to ensure that the goats remain on a sturdy surface all night long.

There is another advantage of having sleeping shelves, besides making a good resting space, which is that the kids will have a safe space where they will not get trampled or hurt. If these kids are not sleeping with their moms, they can also sleep under the shelves to stay protected always.

Waterer

You must ensure that goats are never kept without water. Many goat owners have a misconception that goats may drink too much water and actually die. Hence they keep the waterers away from the goats while feeding them.

This practice is never recommended as goats require water more than food. Especially when you are feeding the goats dry pellets, you must make sure that you provide water alongside it.

When goats eat dry pellets or crumbs and fail to have an adequate amount of water, the feed begins to swell inside the animal. The risk of choking is also high when goats are given dry food without water. So, make sure that you always have enough clean drinking water for the goats.

Feeders

The biggest challenge with goats is to monitor their feed and to make sure that they eat regularly. If you are not able to do this hands on, you can use a food dispenser that works quite well.

The most basic type of food dispenser consists of a plastic dome like structure that has a roof to keep the food dry. It has a small feeder around it where the goats can eat. The beauty of this dispenser is that it keeps refilling the feeder as the goats finish eating. So, all you need to do is fill the dispenser regularly and be care free.

Another interesting type of food dispenser is the tread plate feeder. With this type of feeder, a metal tread plate provides access to the food. Every time a goat steps on this feeder, it will open the lid to the container which stores the feed.

An automatic pet feeder is only useful when you have smaller herds. These feeders are ideal to feed one or two pets each time. So if you have between 2 to 4 goats, this type of feeder might work well for you.

Automatic pet feeders have been designed for people who are unable to stay at home all day to ensure that their pets are being fed on time. It is possible to program close to 10 meals each day for your goat. You can set the program to dispense an exact amount of feed each time. You also have the option of setting different portions each time.

You can time these automatic feeders and be assured that your pet goats will not remain hungry. Like I mentioned before, goats are not really dependent on their owners for their food. They can easily forage around for their food.

In case you have to keep your goat indoors for some reason, this type of feeder works best. For instance, if your goat has undergone any surgery or is under treatment, he may not be able to forage. In such cases an automatic dispenser works best.

Besides making your life easier, food dispensers serve several other purposes. Now, goats poop so often. Undoubtedly, they also remain hungry all the time and constantly require food. With a food dispenser you can ensure that your precious pets have access to food all the time.

A common problem that most goat owners face is finding poop in the food very often. Using a food dispenser puts an end to this rather difficult problem. Also, you will not have to deal with upturned bowls of food. This reduces wastage and ensures that the food is stored in hygienic conditions.

7. Cleaning housing area

A clean housing area is essential for proper hygiene. If you have kids, pregnant goats or animals with a low body condition, you need to be extra cautious as they have very little immunity towards infections and illnesses.

The housing area can get dirty really fast considering that there is going to be a lot of manure and other debris that gets accumulated over time. While you can have a bedding material that is absorbent, it is necessary to change it and clean the housing area regularly.

If there are any organisms in the housing area, there is also a chance that the milk that you consume will get contaminated. Then the shelf life of milk reduces and it may even transmit diseases to the people who consume the milk.

The floor needs to be kept dry at all times to make sure that the animals do not get any foot infection or injury. Insects are also a health hazard. It disturbs the animals to begin with and also spreads diseases in the herd very fast.

How to clean the shed

You need to be willing to use water liberally to thoroughly clean a goat's housing area. You need to have the right equipment such as a wheel barrow in order to lift and dispose the bedding and the dung after it has been cleaned. The housing area needs good drainage so that you can remove liquid waste properly.

It is a good idea to remove fodder and feed that is remaining in the manger. This will reduce any chance of fly related nuisance. When you clean the entire area with water periodically, you can eliminate bacteria, algae, any chance of viral contamination or fungi. That way you can prevent most health issues that goats are prone to.

Which sanitizer to use

One of the best and most potent sanitizers is sunlight. It has the ability to destroy all organisms that produce diseases. The goal of disinfecting a shed is to make it free from any microbes that cause diseases. You can sprinkle the area with the following chemical agents for best results:

- **Bleaching powder:** This compound consists of almost 39% calcium. It is one of the best and most easily available chemicals.

- **Iodophor and iodine:** You can look for commercially made iodophore. This contains 2% iodine and is very effective against germs.

- **Sodium carbonate:** If you decide to use this disinfectant, you can use a hot solution containing 4% sodium carbonate. It will wash away certain strains of bacteria and several viruses.

- **Slaked lime and quick lime:** These ingredients are used to whitewash the walls of the housing area. They prevent several microbes from breeding in the first place.

- **Phenol:** Also known as carbolic acid, this is a common household disinfectant that also works against fungus along with several strains of bacteria.

- **Insecticides:** As the name suggests, these chemicals are effective against insects such as ticks and fleas that normally transmit diseases. You can use insecticides on the crevices of walls and cracks as well. You can make solution of these insecticides and use them to spray and disinfect the most common harboring areas for these insects. Using a powerful sprayer works best, although you can use a brush, sponge or a hand sprayer. The commonly used insecticides are gramazane powder, BHC, DDT, surriithion and malathion. Making a 50% concentrate solution is recommended. However, these insecticides can also be poisonous to livestock. So take care that they do not come in contact with milk, water or any food material.

The right cleaning procedure

- First, the dung should be removed from the urine channel and the floor. You can use an iron basket and a shovel to pick the dung up. Then transfer it on to a wheel barrow. While doing this, also remove any leftovers or bedding material.

- The water trough should be emptied. A floor brush should be used to scrape the bottom and the sides.

- The water trough should then be washed with clean water. It is recommended that you white wash the water trough with the above mentioned lime solution.

- The floor of the housing area must be scrubbed clean using a broom and a brush. Then you can wash it off with water.

- There may be splashes of dung on the wall, poles, railing and other structures. This should be scrubbed and cleaned fully.

- If there are any cobwebs, remove them with a wall brush. You must remove cobwebs periodically to prevent any allergic reaction.

- Once the housing area has been washed thoroughly, you can use disinfecting agents like phenol, bleaching powder or baking soda to sprinkle the whole surface.

Precautions

To make sure that the cleaning process is safe, here are a few tips that you can use:

- The bedding material and the dung should be removed completely.

- If any dung or bedding material spills when you are carrying it out, make sure that you clean it up instantly.

- Dirty water should never be used to clean the shed.

- If there is any fodder left over, clean it before replacing it with fresh fodder. Never put fresh fodder over the left overs.

- Watch for any growth of algae in the water troughs.

- The concentration of the disinfectants should be correct to make sure that they are actually effective. You also need the right concentration to prevent any chances of poisoning or toxicosis in livestock.

Before you add the new bedding material, make sure that the housing area is fully dry. During the rainy season, it is a good idea to spray insecticide regularly. This will keep flies at bay. You may even consider whitewashing regularly to keep the mites and ticks in the walls at bay.

Cleaning the housing area once every week is recommended. If not, you must at least clear out the bedding material and wash the housing area thoroughly every fifteen days. This will prevent any unpleasant odor in the area. The more frequently you clean, the easier it is each time.

Chapter 5: Breeding and Reproduction in Nigerian dwarf goats

With miniature livestock, there are several breeding programs that are available. There are continuous attempts to create new breeds of miniature livestock. But, if you are a novice with Nigerian dwarf goats, the first thing that you need to learn is to identify sexual behavior, take care of the pregnant goat and then ensure safe calving.

1. Sexual behavior in livestock

On average, miniature livestock live up to 12-14 years of age. They will become sexually mature when they are about 12-14 months old. Thereon, your goat will be able to have one billy every year. In case of kids, they are sexually active until the age of 17.

When the goat goes into heat or estrus, the billy in your herd will also become excited. He will stay close to the goat and will often be seen smelling the genital area of the goat.

This is a natural way of transferring pheromones. You will see other behavior such as resting the chin on the rump of the goat, snorting and pawing the ground. This behavior indicates that the billy is going to copulate with the goat in some time. The copulation itself lasts for a few seconds.

If you have a herd, there is a social ranking within it in most cases. The goats that are most dominant will display maximum mating.

You will be able to identify a goat in heat because she will get very excited. Then, there will be several attempts made by the billy to mount her. The level of excitement when the goat is in heat can either be strong, weak or medium. The difference lies in the breed of the goat, the age and just the individual personality of the animal.

If there are castrated Nigerian dwarf kids in your herd, they will display sexual behavior that is similar to the intact ones. However, he will not be able to copulate because the androgens in the body are not present.

In the case of females, the endocrine balance determines the type of behavior exhibited. Now, there are several ovarian secretions that will determine the behavior. But, estrogen plays the most important role with respect to this.

There are many other factors that determine the level of sexual behavior such as the environment, genetics, the health of the animal, physiological factors and the past experiences. If you have new herd members, goats or kids, they will get more sexual attention.

So if you have a billy that is not displaying proper breeding behavior, you can introduce a new member to the herd. If all the kids are sexually healthy, introducing a new animal during the breeding season is never recommended.

The sexual receptivity remains for about 19 hours. When the goats are receptive, they may mount other goats or they may be mounted by other goats as well. When the female is being mounted, she gets into a rigid stance and the process is complete in less than a few seconds.

The gestation period of a Nigerian dwarf goat lasts for 285 days which is the same as the regular sized goat. During this period, proper care and nutrition is necessary. If your goat is giving birth for the first time, the term used to describe her is "heifer".

2. Caring for pregnant goat

A pregnant goat should be kept in a separate enclosure during the third trimester. Nutrition in the pregnant goat is very important to make sure that the billy develops properly. It is also essential to prevent possible diseases like Bovine Respiratory disease in the billy that is born.

On most farms, the common practice is to reduce feed costs with low cost feed. You definitely do not want to do that to your pet, especially when she is pregnant. You need to make sure that she gets the necessary amount of protein, carbohydrates, macro and micro nutrients.

According to the National Research Council, low quality hay does not provide the amount of protein that is necessary for a lactating or pregnant goat.

In addition to this, when the protein level is reduced, the goat may even reduce the intake of food because of an inefficiency of digestion as the rumen microbial populations are unable to perform efficiently.

When the food intake is reduced, the amount of energy that the goat gets is also reduced, leading to poor development of the fetus.

You need to understand how to check for the quality of the food and combine the feed in such a way that the nutritional requirements are fully met. In case you figure out that the food that you are providing is not able to provide the required nutrients, you can even consult your vet to figure out strategies to provide supplementation.

Importance of protein

It has been noticed that when a goat is provided with low quality forage, it leads to a lot of nutritional imbalance. In general, it contains less than 7% protein. If your dwarf belongs to a meat producing breed, the protein requirement is much higher.

In the case of goats, they cannot provide maximum performance if the protein in their body is inadequate.

If you figure out that the quality of fodder that you are providing is low, then you will have to give the goat a protein supplement in the later part of the pregnancy to ensure that the nutrient requirements are met.

Mineral nutrition

The metabolism of a goat can only be sustained if she is able to get enough micro and macro nutrients. They play a very important role in the formation of bones, are important components in the hormones and result in the secretion of hormones, maintenance of water balance and amino acid components. They also act as anti-oxidants.

Goats need at least 17 different minerals including Zinc, chromium, selenium, iron, manganese among others, just before calving.

Although this has not been investigated thoroughly, it is suggested that the immunity of the billy can be compromised to a large extent if the pregnant goat does not have access to these minerals. This increases the incidence of diseases like Bovine Respiratory Disorder.

The forage that you supply accounts for a part of the mineral requirement of goats. If there is any deficiency, it can be managed with mineral supplements that are recommended by the vet. The level of trace minerals in the blood can be evaluated to monitor the level of deficiency in the goat before calving.

Although there is no solid evidence to suggest that nutrition and immune function of the billy are interrelated, it has been concluded that the improper secretion of antibodies and hormones in the billy can compromise the immune system.

The colostrum or "first milk" after the billy is born transfers a lot of immunoglobulins to the billy. This helps prevent diseases and keeps the billy protected for at least 24 hours after birth. If the billy is not given the colostrum, they are at a risk of developing several complications that will lead to poor body conditions and expensive treatment procedures as well.

Besides proper nutrition, you will also have to make the environment of the pregnant goat free from any stressors. This includes noises or other animals. You must provide her with a quiet corner. This is especially needed in the last trimester when the goat can start to get a little uncomfortable.

When your goat is ready to give birth, it is best that you leave her alone and let nature take its course. Sometimes, the goat may need assistance. We will discuss about how you can help deliver the billy. In case you are unsure of this, you can speak to your vet for more assistance.

3. Birthing process

The first and most important thing that you need to do when your goat approaches the time of delivery is to keep her in a secluded barn or housing area. If not, you will have to look around for her all over the property. When goats do not have a warm and quiet birthing area, they will find one themselves.

It is a challenge to look for the goat or heifer when she goes into reclusion on her own. It is also not the best thing to do to approach a goat who is trying to get some peace and quiet. With a barn where she is familiar with your movements, she will be much calmer.

Then, you will observe what stage of birthing she is in. If it is only the first stage, you will see her standing up and pacing around. She will lay down and get up several times.

If you can get close enough, you will see the water sac hanging from the birth canal. It will be yellowish in colour. Usually, immediately after the appearance of this spherical sac, the feet of the billy begin emerging.

The feet should be pointing toward the ground. If not, you are having a breached birth. Observe the goat after the feet start to emerge. If she is able to push the billy out on her own, then it is best that you let her do so. If you see that after the feet have emerged, she has stayed in the same position for more than an hour, you may have to provide necessary assistance to pull the billy out.

You may or may not have to restrain her. If the goat is sitting and settled, you should be able to pull the billy out without any hassle. But, if she is standing and you are not sure if she is tame enough, you can restrain her for your safety.

Using a head gate is the best possible option. If you do not have one, you can get a 10' gate to restrain her. The head gate is recommended as it will prevent any accident or damage if the goat begins to panic and decides to back on you.

You will need a pair of shoulder gloves for hygiene purposes. Start by washing your hands from the shoulder to the fingertips. Then put the gloves on when your hands are fully dry.

It is necessary to apply some lubricant on the gloves to reach in and help pull the billy out. You can try a vet recommended lubricant or can use petroleum jelly. You may have to reach into the birth canal to check on the position of the billy.

Depending on the position of the billy, you will be able to provide the right kind of assistance to the goat. Here are some positions that you can expect:

- Backward position: In this case, you do not have to turn the billy around. You will have to wait till the hind legs of the billy are presented before you provide any assistance. You will use a calving chain or any flexible rope that can be fastened to the billy in order to pull it out as quickly as possible.

- Breach position: This is when the billy is going to be born tail first. This is when you have to get the billy into the correct position to avoid any complications. Push the billy into the uterus as much as possible. The flexed hock will then be pushed away from the billy. The fetlock on the foot should be pushed back inward. Hold the hock joints and the fetlock tight and bring the foot over the pelvic brim into the birth canal. This should be done for both the legs. After that you can tie the rope or the calving chain and begin to pull the billy out.

- Head down or head back position: The billy must be pushed back into the uterine cavity. With one hand hold the billy stable and cup the other one over the nose of the billy. If you are unable to hold on to the head, you can even hook two fingers to the corner of the mouth to get a grip.

Once you have hold of the billy, you will turn him around to the normal position to make the birthing process simple.

- Foreleg back position: The billy will be pushed back in to the uterus. Then, grab the upper leg and pull the billy forward enough to allow the knee to reach forward. Tightly flex the knee and pull forward. After you have flexed the knee tightly, you will cup the hoof with the hand and then bring it to a normal position.
- Bent toe or caught elbow position: The billy should be pushed back into the uterine canal to adjust the position of the elbow and foot. If there is a caught elbow, you can grab the leg that is shoved further up and then pull it forward. As soon as you correct this, the billy will come out quite easily.

Once the billy is in the normal position that you can pull it out from, you can use a rope or a calving chain around the front leg of the billy and then pull it out. It is best that you use a double half hitch knot.

You can put one loop on the fetlock and the other one just below the knee. When the goat is straining, you will pull. When the goat begins to rest, you need to stop pulling, too.

If a billy puller is available to you, make use of it. It will help you prevent pulling the billy out too quickly and causing damage. The billy puller us a U-shaped part that is used on the rear of the goat to attach the chain and pull the billy out. The puller is used at the base of the tail while the chain is attached to the legs of the billy.

As you pull the billy, you can tighten the rope or chain enough to get the billy out easily. When you feel that the tension is good enough to get the billy out, you can work in the same rhythm as the contractions of the goat. Keep increasing the tension as needed to get a better grip.

At one point you will notice that the puller is no longer needed. This is usually when the billy is half way out. Then you can unhook the chain and then pull the billy out by hand.

As soon as the billy is born, the first thing that you need to do is assist it to breathe. The nose should be cleaned out using your finger to get the amniotic fluid out. Follow this with a gentle tickle in the nose using a piece of hay.

You can also put a few drops of water in the ears to get the billy to shake its head. In extreme cases, you will have to provide artificial respiration to make the billy breathe. Ideally, a billy should breathe within 60 seconds of being born.

The billy should be shifted to a new pen which has clean straw as bedding. After that, you can let the mother enter the area and spend time with the little one.

The mother and the newborn billy should be allowed to rest in a quiet area. The mother will lick the billy clean and then persuade him to begin nursing. The mother goat needs a good amount of hay and clean water to relax after the strenuous birthing process.

Make sure that you keep her area clear of any disturbances such as a sudden sound or even too much activity.

4. Mother and billy behavior

Just between 2-5 hours after birth, suckling behavior starts as long as the mother is standing. The billy will butt at the udder of the mother when he is learning to suckle. Heifers take more time to stand as the first birth is always difficult. Experienced goats will stand up much faster.

In order to stimulate breathing, the mother will lick the billy constantly. This simulates circulation and also excretion. It is common for the goat to hide the billy as an instinct. This is to prevent predators from attacking the helpless young billy. The goat will probably showcase this behavior even when she is on your farm.

Suckling begins with the front teat normally. It is most intense as soon as the billy stands up. The billy and the mother continue to increase the distance between them after calving. After some time, they will begin to communicate by vocalizing.

In the first week, the billy will follow the goat. If you have a herd, you will notice that the kids form a group of their own and stay in that group while the goats graze. This group is called a nursery and is an indication that the kids will begin to graze on their own soon.

You may even have a guard goat who will observe the behavior of the kids in the initial period. Goats are also ready to foster other kids when they are nursing. The number of kids that are nursed varies from one goat to the other.

If you removed the kids from the mother as soon as they are weaned, you can condition them better. This will help you get them used to human handling and will also be able to take care of procedures like dehorning, castration and others. They will be quieter and easier to handle as they age.

When they are constantly in human contact, they will be less stressed when they are expected to do so at a later age. If the billy is left with the mother, they may be taught to avoid human interaction as a behavior. They will pick up other behavior as well that will make them hard to handle.

The mother goat uses the vocal, visual and olfactory senses to identify the billy. When a goat begins to groom the billy, she labels the billy as her own. In most cases, the billy will stand up in just 45 minutes of being born.

The mother will aid suckling by adjusting her body in a way that is easier for the little one to access. Until 7 months from being born, the suckling time of the billy is about 34 minutes.

The frequency is between 4 to 5 times per day. Studies have revealed that heifers or female kids are weaned at the age of 8 months while kids are weaned at the age of 11 months.

The mother and the child should have a dry and soft surface to rest on. Then the billy will be cleaned by the mother. If you find that she is licking the billy for too long, it is good to separate the two so that the billy has more time to nurse and feed with the mother. The hormonal activity in the body of the mother will determine her maternal behavior.

You cannot really predict maternal behavior in goats. So, one that makes a great mother may not necessary produce a heifer who has the same maternal behavior.

But, the bond between the mother and the billy is quite strong. Within just five minutes of being born, the mother and the billy will develop a specific maternal bond that helps the mother identify, nurture and protect her little one.

But sometimes, there can be abnormal maternal behaviors that you need to have checked by a vet. If left unattended, such kids may be in danger of being injured or staying malnourished as the mother refuses to feed them.

5. Abnormal breeding behavior

There are some behavior patterns in the goat that you should watch out for. If the misbehavior is targeted towards the billy, you must seek professional help. It may even help to find a foster for the newborn.

Mismothering: This is usually noticed in goats that are in a very intensely managed maternity group. In a very difficult birth that could have been long and painful, the mother will not stand up for suckling. Even the billy may be too weak to suckle.

Allowing an experienced goat to foster the billy may work. If you do not have than option, hand feeding is the next best alternative.

Nymphomania: Yes, it is possible for your livestock to exhibit this behavior. If the goat belongs to a breed, this behavior is more common. You will see that the goat begins to behave like a billy.

She will begin to paw and will mount other goats or will simply not allow a billy or another goat to mount her. She may even become aggressive. Nymphomania has been associated with cysts in the follicles.

Billyer-steer syndrome: If the goat is raised in an improper feedlot set up, she will display this health problem. This behavior tends to attract many kids who will mount the goat taking turns.

This leads to serious injuries and the billyer needs to be segregated from a herd. Almost 2% of the steers in a feedlot tend to display this health concern.

Illnesses: If your livestock has any health issues, it will lead to abnormal behavior. A goat that is healthy will be alert at all times, will be vocal and will display behavior like stretching when they get up after a period of complete rest. But, an unwell goat will not move fast, will have dull eyes and will seem to be disinterested in the environment.

They may also stop eating and nursing. There are several other indications of poor health including teeth grinding and hunching the back. We will discuss this in detail in the following chapter.

There are options to normalize and modify this behavior through procedures like endocrine implants. It is also easier to handle livestock that has been neutered or spayed. If you are not interested in breeding your Nigerian dwarf goat, you can get them neutered at a young age to avoid these behaviors.

Normally, sexual behavior that is not ordinary is the result of endocrine imbalances, genetic issues and also poor management. The good news is that you can reverse most of this behavior with help from proper professionals.

It will also help to learn more about breeding behavior and general livestock behavior to make the environment less stressful for your goat.

In the breeding season, especially, the surge of hormones may lead to difficulty in handling your Nigerian dwarf goat. But with some patience and knowledge, you should be able to manage most situations effectively.

6. Raising kids

Taking care of a newborn billy is no piece of cake. You will require a lot of patience to make sure that the billy is comfortable and is developing properly.

There are several reasons why you may have to take on this role. The mother may succumb to a difficult birthing process, she may develop abnormal behavior or you may just prefer to have a billy that is hand raised. It is best that you handle the billy after it has been weaned. But, if you have to take care of a newborn billy, here are a few tips and techniques.

Rearing a newborn billy

If a newborn billy has been orphaned, you will notice depression, dehydration and a loss of appetite. You will have to provide proper care for the first 24 hours to make sure that the billy is healthy and to ensure survival.

Colostrum is needed for the newborn billy in order to be healthy. This is the first milk that is produced by the mother. Passive immunity against possible health threats is provided with the colostrum which is rich in minerals and vitamins.

In the first 36 hours of being born, it is necessary for the billy to get this colostrum. You can either get it from the mother or can opt for artificial sources.

If you have several goats in your herd that are calving, it is advised that you take one portion of the colostrum and freeze it. You can look for milk replacers that contain colostrum as well.

As soon as the billy has consumed the colostrum, he can be given whole milk or a milk replacer. If you have frozen colostrum, you can hand feed the baby.

It should be warmed to 36 degrees before you feed it to the billy. In case you have a good supply of colostrum available, you can feed it to the billy for the first two days.

You must give him two feeds, one in the morning and one in the evening. Each portion should consist of at least 2 liters of colostrum for it to have the desired effect on the development of the billy.

If the billy is born dehydrated, you will have to rehydrate it before feeding. A billy that is dehydrated will have scours or may not even survive if he is given milk before rehydration. You can make an electrolyte mixture at home or can purchase one from the vet.

At home, electrolytes can be made by adding ½ teaspoon of baking soda, 1 teaspoon of table salt and 125g of glucose to about 1.2litres of water. Before you give the billy any milk, make sure that he has received the electrolyte for at least 24 hours to rehydrate completely.

Feeding options

Livestock have four stomachs and are called ruminants. When the billy is born, only the fourth stomach or the abomasum is the one that is functioning. It is harder to feed a billy with teats but when the billy suckles, the esophageal groove responds by closing and directing the milk directly to the fourth stomach where it is easily digested.

Using teats will also stimulate the production of saliva and will urge the billy to take in more fluids. The teats should be kept clean at all times and if there is any deterioration in the condition of the teat, it must be replaced.

You have the option of using a bucket to feed the billy as well. But the issue with the bucket is that the esophageal reflex is never triggered and the milk will go straight to the rumen.

The rumen is not functioning at this point and the milk stays undigested. This leads to scouring or diarrhea in the kids.

When you use a bucket, you need to make sure that it is at least 30cms above the ground. This will help the groove close and prevent the milk from entering the rumen.

If your billy does not take to the bucket instantly, you will have to train him to do so. Straddle the neck with the billy backed into a corner. Moisten your fingers with milk and take it to the mouth of the billy.

No matter what method you use, the billy should be given a measured amount of milk. When the billy gets older, he will begin to graze. Then, the other stomachs will begin to develop. So, you need to make sure that your billy has a good amount of high quality hay in order to stimulate the proper development of the rumen.

Controlling illnesses

One of the most common issues in young kids is scouring or diarrhea. This can lead to death very quickly if not treated properly. When you notice this in a billy, make sure that he is taken off milk for a minimum of four hours during which he is provided with a good amount of electrolytes.

In case scouring continues after this, you will need proper medication to help the billy. This should be provided only after consulting the vet.

When you are expecting a billy, keeping this scouring medicine handy can save the newborn's life. Make sure that the sick billy is isolated.

You must always keep the environment of the billy hygienic. If you are using teats, make sure that it is cleaned properly and is maintained in good condition. This is one of the best ways to prevent any illness in hand raised kids.

The billy must always have ample water to drink. This will keep them healthy. Kids will not drink any water up to two weeks of age. By the time they are six weeks old, they will be consuming almost five liters of water each day. You cannot expect water to be replaced with milk even if you are feeding the billy twice a day.

The water bowl needs to be cleaned regularly as the billy may foul it while feeding. You must also allow the billy to interact with older ones that have a fully developed rumen. This will help them pick up some necessary microbes that aid digestion of food in the rumen.

They are passed on from one billy to the other when they graze on the same pasture. They can also be spread through behavior like licking which is very common when kids are being introduced to one another, almost like an approval.

Feeding a kid or billy

- If you are using milk replacers, make sure that they contain 10% fat, 20% protein and not more than 10% of starch and sugar. Reconstitute the feed and provide it as per the instructions given by the manufacturer.

- You can increase the portion of the powder if you are feeding the kids only once in order to reduce the volume of food required.

- If you are feeding more than one billy, you will draft them as per the feeding habit.

- Milk should be divided into separate feeds. One can be given in the morning and the other in the evening at a regular time.

- As the billy grows and begins to forage, you can give him one feed a day. Make sure that he has a lot of cool and fresh water to drink at this stage.

- Good hygiene is a must when you are hand-raising a billy.

- You must never over feed a billy. This is especially important in the first three weeks of their life as it may lead to diarrhea or scouring. You must feed a billy 10% of his body weight every day. For example, if the billy weighs about 20 kilos you will provide 2L of milk every day.

- The milk should be at a temperature between 35 to 38 degrees.

- Clean water should be provided at all times. The water trough should be cleaned out regularly to prevent the chance of any diseases.

- You must never alter the amount of feed that you are giving the billy suddenly.

- As kids get older, they will need more food. Milk replacer is an expensive option. It is a better idea to make up for the required volume of food with grain and pellet.

- You can make this available at all times. They will feed on their own and will slowly increase the amount of grain that they consume. This will make it a lot easier for you to wean the billy when the time comes.

- When you switch to solid foods, make sure that good quality hay is introduced along with concentrates when the billy is about two weeks old.

Weaning a billy

- You can wean a billy more easily at a younger age. Providing milk up to 12 weeks of age is good enough as long as the billy is in good health and is developing properly.

- If you introduce grains and solid food when the billy is about one week old, you will be able to wean him off milk completely by the time he is five weeks old.

- You must wean the billy as per the consumption of concentrate. When the billy is consuming at least 650g of food in a day you should wean him.

- Do not use age as a basis to wean the billy. In some cases, the billy will be able to reach this target earlier.

- You can reduce the milk concentration over a week to make weaning quicker and more abrupt.

- You will have to provide the weaned billy with good management. Otherwise, poor nutrition and poor management will lead to stunted growth that cannot be reversed.

- In the case of young kids, the diet should contain at least 20% of crude proteins.

- Make sure you provide fresh feed every day and clean out any leftovers from the trough every time you feed.

Providing solid food

- When the billy is about one week old, you can start by providing access to clean hay all day.

- This will improve the activity of the rumen. By the time the billy is about 12 weeks old, the rumen should be functioning normally.

- You will only give them high quality baby billy meals or good quality pellet till they are about five weeks old.

- Green grass in excess should be avoided till the billy is 6 weeks old to prevent any indigestion.

- You can provide concentrates to the goat by adding a little to the milking bucket. Just when the billy is about to finish drinking the milk, you can rub some concentrate on the muzzle. This will encourage them to taste it.

- By the time the billy is three weeks old, you can give him hay, grain and access to green pasture in small amounts. Any change that you make in the feed should be gradual.

- As per the quality of the pasture, you may have to provide the billy with concentrates and supplementary hay until the billy reaches the desired body weight.

- The concentrate that you provide to your billy should have a coarse texture, should be highly palatable and should provide the billy with proteins, roughage and a lot of energy.

- A good mix includes four parts of crushed grain and one part of linseed, peanut, cottonseed meal or copra. You can also add a small amount of molasses to it to make the billy relish it more.

- You can add rumen modifiers as advised by the vet. This will improve the activity of the rumen and will also prevent any chances of coccidiosis in kids.

- You can add this as per the instructions by the manufacturer. It can be added to pellets, molasses based food mix and also pre-mixed meals. You must not add it to any urea based supplement.

- Rumen modifiers should be provided in small quantities as an excess can be toxic.

- You can provide protein meals as a natural source of bypass and rumen degradable proteins.

- You must never provide non protein sources of nitrogen such as urea when the billy is very young.

- The best hay for a young billy is Lucerne hay. It should be checked for any weed or mold before feeding it to the kids.

- In case you have a pasture that is scarce or is not of good quality, supplementing the feed with good quality hay will work wonders.

As discussed, rearing and hand raising kids can be a difficult task. The goal must always be healthy development of your pet and if you have any queries, you can speak to your vet for more suggestions.

Chapter 6: Diet requirements of the Nigerian dwarf goat

As the owner or as the prospective owner of a Nigerian dwarf goat, it should be your foremost concern to provide adequate and proper nutrition to the pet. If the pet animal is deficient in any nutrient, he will develop various deficiencies and acquire many diseases. When the nutrition is right, you can easily ward off many dangerous diseases.

Each animal species is different. Just because certain kinds of foods are good for your pet dog, it does not mean that they will be good for your pet Nigerian dwarf goat also.

It is important to learn about all the foods that the Nigerian dwarf goats are naturally inclined towards eating. You should always be looking at maintaining good health of your pet.

It is important to learn about the foods that are good for your Nigerian dwarf goat. But, you should also understand that the foods that you feed your pet with could be lacking in certain nutrients. An animal in the wild is different from one in captivity. Availability of certain foods will also affect the diet of your pet.

Generally, the food given to captive pets is lacking in certain nutrients. It is not able to provide the pet with all the necessary nutrients. Im such a case, you will have to give commercial pellets to your Nigerian dwarf goat. These pellets are known to compensate for the various nutritional deficiencies that the animal might have due to malnutrition.

You should always aim at providing wholesome nutrition to your pet. It is important to understand the pet's nutritional requirements and include all the nutrients in his daily meals. To meet his nutritional requirements, you might also have to give him certain supplements.

The supplements will help you to make up for the essential nutrients that are not found in his daily meals. Though these supplements are easily available, you should definitely consult a veterinarian before you give your Nigerian dwarf goat any kind of supplements.

It is very important that you serve only high quality food to your pet. If you are trying to save some money by buying cheaper low quality alternatives, then you are in a bad situation. A low quality food will affect the health of the Nigerian dwarf goat.

You can expect him to acquire deficiencies and diseases when he is not fed good quality food. The cure is taking the pet to the veterinarian. This in turn will only cost you more money. To avoid this endless loop, it is better to work on the basics. Keep the pet healthy by feeding him with high quality foods, rather than spending money on him by taking him to the veterinarian.

Maintaining the health of your livestock comes from good husbandry and care. There are a few things that form the basics of proper livestock care and you need to ensure that you take care of everything to keep your heard safe and healthy.

Here are some tips to provide best possible care to your beloved miniature livestock.

1. Feeding miniature livestock

You must always stock up on the food supplies to ensure that you don't compromise on the nutrition of your goats. It is true that goats will eat just about anything. In fact, you must allow them to forage around and graze.

This is a very important part of their natural behaviour. However, if you are housing a herd or even pet goats, you must control their diet to an extent to make sure that they are healthy.

Grazing ads a lot of supplements to your goats diet, no doubt. Just like any other animal in their family, goats love to eat woody weeds, bushes and trees. They will also taste a bit of everything.

However, this must be controlled as much as you can as grazing puts the goats at the risk of consuming harmful parasites. So, you must feed them enough to make sure that they do not graze too often.

Goats need certain important nutrients in order to produce good products like milk. For those who are interested in showing the goats, you must be extra careful with what you feed the goat. You must not allow the quality of the hair to reduce or even allow your goat to become obese.

You have to first assess the requirements of your livestock to make sure that they are getting what their body demands. Here are a few factors that you must consider:

Depending on what is naturally available to these animals in their local environment, you can prepare a nutritious meal plan for them. The local environment also affects the demands and the water requirements.

The climatic changes affect the animal based on the thickness of the hide, the hair condition and the depth of the hair.

There are two options when it comes to feeding your livestock, you can either stick to dry lot feeding where the food is harvested and stored before giving it to your livestock. The next option is to let the livestock graze if you have a large enough pasture.

With dry-lot livestock if you are unable to offer a bedding of straw or sawdust and provide mud instead, it will affect the level of consumption to a large extent. However, the nutrition requirements should be kept in mind irrespective of the kind of feed you offer.

2. What to feed your livestock

Essentially, livestock are anatomically designed to consume grass or roughage. Grain feeding involves providing livestock with a certain ration that consists of a mix of different grains.

For a balanced meal, it is a good idea to allow the animals to graze at least once a day and then provide them with a grain mix or hay and alfalfa grass. While nutritionally, grass feeding and grain feeding will not have too much difference, the latter makes the livestock stressed as it is far removed from their normal biological need. Therefore, a mix or adding supplements to grazing livestock is recommended.

Alfalfa and hay

If you live in an area where there are significant non-grazing seasons, hay and alfalfa can become the main source of nutrients for your goats. Hay or alfalfa provides the goats with protein and a good dose of energy.

Alfalfa is called legume hay and is more beneficial to your goat's health. In addition to high amounts of protein, they also contain calcium, vitamins and other minerals. You must provide your goats with specially stored and cured hay for best results.

On an average, a goat will require about 4 pounds of hay every day. You should either make it available all day or make sure that the goats are fed twice each day even when the goats are browsing.

You also get alfalfa pellets that you can mix with the grains. This makes it easy to store and also reduces wastage.

Chaffhaye

Chaffhaye is a great substitute for grass hay. You can use early grass or alfalfa to make this. All you need is to chop the grass or alfalfa, spray with some molasses and add store bought culture of bacillus subtillis. Then, you need to vacuum pack the mixture. This hay will ferment in the bag. The bacterial culture that you add aids digestion in goats.

This is a great source of minerals, vitamins and energy. On average, an adult goat will need about 2 pounds of chaffhaye for every 100 pounds in body weight. The nutritional value of 50 pounds of chaffhaye is equal to 100 pounds of high quality hay.

Grains

Pellet grain mixes or grains are great for your goat's diet. They provide minerals, vitamins and proteins. You can even give your goat store bought grain pellets that are formulated specially to provide nutrition to goats. These are the grain options that you can choose from:

Whole grain: this includes unprocessed seed heads of grains.

Pelleted grain: these products are made from whole grains or grain by products that are broken into smaller pieces and then bound into pellets using a special agent.

Rolled grain: Rolled grain is similar to whole grain. It is different in shape and is flat because it has been rolled.

Texturized grain: This is similar to the previous option. The difference is that there are other ingredients that have been mixed with it to improve the health benefits.

Besides these regular foods, you must also provide your goats with supplements and medicated feed. This is extremely important if you are commercially rearing goats. You will also have to find good supplements if you have a pregnant doe or even an unwell goat at home.

Now, you can feed livestock twice a day. Keep the feeding time consistent and make sure that there is a gap of 12 hours between each feed. During the summer, their appetite will decrease and it will help to provide the first feed earlier in the morning. You must also make sure that the livestock is eating well. Ideally, the food that you provide should be consumed within 30 minutes, indicating a healthy eating habit.

3. Ideal feeding routine

Good nutrition is the key to preventing several diseases. You need to have a feeding management practice or a proper routine that will help you do the same.

Most hoof related diseases, that are a major concern for livestock, are related to the feeding frequency and the size of the forages and grains. If you are transitioning your Nigerian dwarf goat to a new diet, putting them into a routine can be one of the key factors in health.

If you have a herd, you must give them a grain mix twice each day. If your goat is milking, you can even increase it to three or four portions as recommended by your vet. This should be followed by foraging on a pasture for at least an hour.

If you are giving your livestock only mixed rations, make sure that you check all the high moisture food thoroughly. These herds must be checked every quarter to ensure that they are getting all the nutrients that are required for them. Make sure that you keep the mix consistent and balanced. Providing grains outside the regular mix means that your goats will begin to have preferences for what they want to eat.

You can also include dietary buffers. You will have to add about 0.8% of the dry matter equivalent to the diet. These buffers will prevent any acidosis in the rumen of your livestock.

The particle size of the forage and the grain is also of great importance. If the particle size in your grain mix or forage is too small and the amount of fiber provided is low, they can lead to serious health issues. You need to distribute the feed and the forage particles in a way that the goats are able to digest properly.

The processing method of the grains and the moisture content in the food also chances the availability of non-fiber carbohydrates. This is a major concern when you do not provide forage with a grain mix.

If you are switching any animal from one diet to another, you need to keep the transition as gradual as possible. For example, when you are changing the diet of a calving goat, you can increase the concentrate of feed to about 0.75 percent of the body weight. Ideally, the animals that are on one type of diet should be divided into a different group with an entirely different ration.

With a smaller body weight, you need to be careful with the portion that you provide your goat with. The nutrients should be balanced. In order to develop properly, goats require vitamins, trace minerals, proteins and carbohydrates. If you are unsure of how to achieve this balance, it is best that you consult your vet.

You may change the routine slightly when the weather changes. Even this should be done gradually to prevent any stress to the animal. Stress always compromises the immune system and provides a gateway for several disease causing microbes.

4. Supplements

The diet of the Nigerian dwarf goat should be highly nutritious. If you make sure that the Nigerian dwarf goat is getting all its necessary nutrients from the food itself, you can avoid the use of supplements. At times, your Nigerian dwarf goat's diet might not be able to provide it with the right set of nutrients and vitamins. In such a case, it becomes necessary to introduce supplements in the diet of the Nigerian dwarf goat.

If the pet is not well and is recuperating from an injury or disease, the veterinarian might advise you to add certain supplements to the pet. These supplements will help the pet to heal faster and get back on his feet sooner.

You should always consult a veterinarian before you give any supplement to the Nigerian dwarf goat. He will be the best judge of which supplements the Nigerian dwarf goat requires and which ones he doesn't.

There are many vitamin supplements that are available in tasty treat forms for the Nigerian dwarf goat. While you can be sure that your pet is getting the right nutrients, the pet can enjoy the treat given to him.

You can also include supplements of fatty acids in the diet of the Nigerian dwarf goat. A few drops of this kind of supplement will enhance the taste and the nutritional value of the food item that is being served to the Nigerian dwarf goat.

While it can be necessary to supplement certain vitamins and nutrients to the pet, you should also be aware of the hazards of over feeding a certain nutrient. If there is an overdose of a certain vitamin in the body of the Nigerian dwarf goat, it can lead to vitamin toxicity.

Another point that you should take care of is that you should not blindly follow the instructions and dosage that is printed on various supplements.

The food that you feed the Nigerian dwarf goat will also have a supply of vitamins. The Nigerian dwarf goat will only require some extra dosage.

Avoid supplements that are labelled "goat/ sheep minerals". These are always low in copper. It is better to use horse minerals or regular cattle minerals instead.

There are some natural supplemental options that you can give your goats too. Some of the most recommended ones are:

Beet Pulp: It is rich in fiber and protein and is also a source of energy. It also contains traces of calcium and phosphorous that is great for the goats. It is best to purchase the 50 pound bags available in stores.

BOSS: Black oil sunflower seeds (BOSS) provide zinc, iron, vitamin E and selenium along with fat and fiber. These supplements add shine to the goat's skin and also improve the butterfat content of the milk. You can just mix these seeds with the grains.

Kelp Meal: This is a good source of iodine and selenium. It reduces the chances of iodine deficiency in goats. This supplement also increases production of dairy including richness of milk and volume of milk produced.

Baking Soda: Several goat owners I know provide baking soda as a free choice mineral to goats. This is useful in improving their digestion and also maintains the pH of the rumen.

Apple Cider Vinegar: ACV contains several enzymes, minerals and vitamins that are useful for goats. You can just add the ACV to your goat's water.

5. Foods to avoid

Here are some foods that you must avoid entirely when it comes to goats:

- Potatoes, tomatoes or any foods with alkaloids. They can be poisonous.
- Avocadoes
- Azalea
- African Rue
- Boxwood
- Brouwer's Beaut
- Burning bush berries
- Calotropis
- China Berry, all parts

- Choke Cherry
- Cassava
- Dumb Cane
- Datura
- Dog Hobble
- False Tansy
- Fusha
- Flizweed
- Holly
- Japanese Yew
- Japanese pieris
- Lakspur
- Lantana
- Lasiandra
- Lilacs
- Lily of the Valley
- Lupine
- Monkwood
- Maya maya
- Milkweed
- Mountain Laurel
- All Nightshade plants
- Rhubarb leaves
- Wild Cherry
- Tu Tu
- Yew

If you find any of these plants growing in your home, you must pluck them out. However, if you have planted them by choice, you must place mesh or fencing around the plant to prevent your goats from eating it.

6. Treats

Any pet loves treats. There are many snacks that are packed with nutrients, including:

- Corn chips that is excellent for the withers because of the high saltiness. This makes them drink more water, preventing chances of calculi in the urine.

- Apples, watermelons, peaches, bananas, grapes and dried fruit are among the favourites of goats. Give them small pieces of these organic fruits to prevent choking.

- Vegetables like carrots, lettuce, pumpkin, spinach and any greens work really well with the goats.

Chapter 7: Health of the Nigerian dwarf goat

An unhealthy pet can be a nightmare for any owner. The last thing that you would want is to see your pet lying down in pain. Many disease causing parasites dwell in unhygienic places and food. If you take care of the hygiene and food of the Nigerian dwarf goat, there are many diseases that you can avert.

At times, even after all the precautions that you take, the pet can get sick. It is always better to be well equipped so that you can help your pet. You should always consult a vet when you find any unusual traits and symptoms in the pet.

You should understand the various health related issues that your pet Nigerian dwarf goat can suffer from. This knowledge will help you to get the right treatment at the right time. It is also important that you understand how you can take care of a sick pet. This knowledge will help you to keep calm and help the sick Nigerian dwarf goat.

Maintaining your Nigerian dwarf goat includes proper care and food. Above all, you need to make sure that your goat is free from any illnesses. You need to be extra cautious as there are several bovine diseases that can also be transmitted to humans through milk or through the environment.

From finding a reliable vet to having a proper program to prevent common illnesses, this chapter will take you through all the aspects of perfect healthcare that you need to provide to your dwarf.

1. Identifying illness in Nigerian dwarf goats

Providing timely assistance is key to maintaining your miniature livestock. Only when you are able to identify a possible illness will you be able to provide the right medication at the right time. Be observant of your dwarf and make sure that you note down any deviation from normalcy. Here are some definite signs that your livestock will display when sick or injured.

Check the body temperature

If you keep a regular tab on the temperature of the goat's body, you will be able to identify an illness almost immediately. In several kids, the best indication of illness is body temperature as they provide very little or confusing visual signs.

The rule of thumb is that any increase in temperature above 104 degrees Fahrenheit in rectal temperature is a sign of illness. Of course, you must never neglect visual signs irrespective of the body temperature of the goat.

The body responds in the most natural manner to disease causing organisms. The immune system prepares to fight the infection, thus causing a temperature surge. In some cases, the goat will be able to overcome the infection on their own and will recover without any signs.

In other cases, you will have a noticeable increase in body temperature along with other visual signs. Neglecting this will lead to worsening of clinical signs and may lead to death if the goat is not treated.

The earlier you detect an elevation in body temperature, the more effective the treatment is.

The biggest problem that you will face with livestock is that there is no "normal" body temperature per say. The body temperature is low in the morning and continues to raise through the day. This heat load is shed fast as nigh time approaches, enough to reach a minimum temperature in the morning. This fluctuation of body temperature occurs even in the colder months.

During day light hours, the temperature will increase even when the temperature of the environment is controlled and maintained at a standard. So it is clear that not only the environment affects the body temperature of goats.

There are several factors like the level of activity, feeding, humidity and solar radiation that affect the body temperature of goats. You will see rapid increase in body temperature after the goat has eaten or after any exercise.

This is the primary reason why livestock must be allowed ample rest after sundown. While it may seem like a good time to take them out to the field, they have to rest in order to let go of the body heat. This is especially true when the day is very hot.

On warm days, it is critical to note the body temperature of the goat in the afternoon. Many farm owners will allow the livestock to rest or just stand for about three hours before they measure the body temperature in the afternoon.

You must also follow this procedure to minimize any form of stress before you take the body temperature.

Visual signs of illness

Suppression of appetite is the first give away of illness in goats. When a goat is exposed to any respiratory disease, her appetite will begin to decrease in just 48 hours from infection. This is long before an elevation in body temperature is noticed.

Make sure that you observe your livestock whenever you feed them. You cannot really monitor them when they are grazing on a daily basis. However, you can make up for this by checking the gut fill of the goat.

If the belly is bouncing as she walks and the goat looks gaunt, it is a sign that she may not be eating as well. She may have also stopped consuming water in the required quantity. If the body condition deteriorates and the weight reduces rapidly, it is an indication of illness.

There are other signs that you need to watch out for including:

- Deep coughing
- Depression
- Drooping head and ears
- Slow movement
- Lagging behind when in a herd
- Reluctance to stand up
- Nasal discharge
- Eye discharge
- Bloody diarrhea

These symptoms are noticed after the animal has stopped feeding properly and after the rectal temperature is high. So, the more you observe your livestock, the faster will you be able to get them the treatment that they need in order to fight an infection.

Sometimes, these signs of illnesses can even be caused by a vaccination provided to the goat. When you put your goat on any vaccination program, be sure to check with the vet about the possible symptoms that you can expect.

That way you will be able to distinguish if the goat is actually ill or whether she is experiencing a temporary side effect caused by the vaccination.

Livestock manure can also be examined to determine whether your goat is sick or not. If the manure is loose and has large particles of feed along with blood and mucus, it can indicate some sort of injury. In the case of a grazing herd, you cannot really separate the specific goat or billy. Then, an abnormality in the manure is a sign for you to become alert and keep an eye on the herd. It is common for a goat to defecate when being handled. Make sure that you keep an eye out for any abnormality when you are doing so.

Identifying injuries

The injuries in livestock can range from minor to severe. Sometimes, it is easy to detect the injury upon observation. These injuries usually manifest in the form of lameness or inability to stand up. With such injuries, it becomes hard to sell a goat. Besides that, you do not have to worry about the general behavior of your pet after she has been treated.

There are other injuries that have more subtle signs and symptoms. These include bruises and any form of organ damage that can be caused with diseases like hardware disease. You can expect such an injury if the animal shows sudden changes in appetite and becomes reluctant to move.

You must examine the immediate environment of the goat to make sure that there aren't any potential hazards that could have led to an injury. The horns of other animals in the herd can also cause a significant amount of bruising. This is most common during breeding season or if you are not providing enough food leading to competition within the herd. If there are any sharp objects such as nails in the handling area and the pastures, they may injure the goat as well.

The key to treating injuries is to observe the animal when you are feeding them or washing them. You can check for any mild lacerations or cuts, blood vessel ruptures, mouth injuries, foot injuries, eye injuries or any damage caused by insect bites. In order to notice these injuries, you will have to make sure that you pay close attention whenever you are handling the animal.

In most cases, this can be treated in your home while keeping the goat restrained. If you are unsure of the type of injury and the treatment, you may have to contact your vet immediately to check the goat.

When you notice that your pet is sick or injured, it should be managed immediately. It is very common for livestock to be put down, on large farms, because the initial symptoms were ignored. You certainly do not want that for your beloved pet dwarf.

Work with your vet to figure out a program or a routine that can keep the health of your dwarf in top shape. If there are any situations that are not included in the plan, you can contact your vet for any assistance. The more you learn about livestock health, the better you will be able to prevent diseases and illnesses in your pet.

2. Common health issues

There are a few diseases that your Nigerian dwarf goat is prone to. If you have raised a regular sized stock, the diseases that affect them will affect a Nigerian dwarf goat as well. Here are some diseases that you must look out for:

Tick borne diseases

- The damage caused by ticks is mostly around the ear and udder area. These wounds tend to get infected and will eventually be attacked by flies.
- Certain ticks like the ones that cause heart water infection tend to cause more damage in livestock than other types of ticks.
- Treating for ticks is necessary every week during the rainy season and every fortnight during the dry season.
- If the goat is vaccinated, then you will be able to treat them less often and still prevent tick borne diseases.
- Ticks will infect livestock with several diseases like gall sickness.
- European breeds tend to be at a greater risk of getting these diseases.
- The older the animal, the greater the risk of tick borne diseases.
- Vaccination and other preventive measures can be taken against tick borne diseases.
- It is best that you have the billy vaccinated before the age of 6 months to make sure that they stay free from tick borne diseases.

Redwater disease

- Redwater is accompanied by symptoms like

    - Red urine

    - Pale and yellow gums

    - Pale eyes

- Loss of appetite

- Nervous signs such as inability to walk.

- The goat may succumb to this condition if not treated appropriately and in time.

- Keeping the livestock free from any stress is a big part of the treatment program. Make sure that you do not graze them over long distances

- It is advised to inject them with Imizol or Berenil.

Heartwater

- The most common signs are:

    - Depression

    - Fever

    - High stepping

    - Convulsions

- When left untreated, death is inevitable with your Nigerian dwarf goat if she is infected with heartwater.

- The best possible treatment is tetracycline.

- With tick borne diseases, proper hygiene and timely care is the best way to prevent any complications. You must also control the insects in the housing area to prevent diseases from spreading from the infected animal to the others. It is a good idea to isolate any goat who has a severe tick infestation.

Tuberculosis

- Sudden weight loss is the most sure shot indication of tuberculosis in livestock.

- A simple skin test can be done every year by the state vet to check if your goat has tuberculosis.

- When an animal is tested positive for tuberculosis, he will be given a T-brand on the neck.

Livestock measles

- This is a type of measles that is caused by tapeworm in livestock. It can infect people only when the meat of an infected animal is consumed.

- Usually livestock will pick up tapeworm eggs when they are grazing. The cause for infestation of the pasture is due to poor toilet practices by people in some areas.

- The measles is not visible in the animal and is normally seen only when the meat is cut.

- Proper hygiene is necessary to keep the animals free from tapeworm infections.

Anthrax

- This disease can lead to sudden death in livestock.

- People catch the infection when they consume the meat and also through cuts and sores on the animal's body.

- If an animal has succumbed to this disease, it is best to bury or burn the carcass.

- The only way to prevent the condition is with proper vaccination.

- In case you have any suspicion of an anthrax infection, you may want to check with your state vet.

Rabies

- This is not a very common condition in livestock but an infection can be caused if the goat is bitten by a rabid dog or jackal.

- The livestock will either be too excited and aggressive or will seem like he has no energy at all.

- If you reach into the goat's mouth for a routine dental examination or if you are bitten by a goat with rabies, you can be infected.

- It is only possible to vaccinate a goat against rabies as there is no cure once the animal has been infected.

Foot related problems

The hoof is one of the most sensitive areas in your goat's body. It is the area that comes in contact with moisture and dirt and when not maintained well, can get seriously infected. Some of the most common foot related issues are:

Laminitis

This is when the dermal layers of the feet have an aseptic inflammation. This leads to sensitivity and inflammation. The symptoms of the condition are:

- Moving in a stiff and cramped manner.
- Standing on the toes while moving to the very edge of the stall is a common way to reduce pain.
- Hemorrhages in the sole.
- Yellow colouration of the sole.
- A white line may appear in the junction between the sole and the wall of the hoof.
- Cracked heels
- Double soles

Sometimes the animal may not show any sign of lameness or pain. While you cannot point to one causal factor, some of the most significant reasons include:

- Increased fermented carbohydrates leading to acidosis of the rumen.
- Poor nutritional management.
- Hormonal changes during parturition or the lactation cycle.
- Digestive or metabolic disorders.
- Infections such as foot rot, meritis and mastitis.
- Hard surfaces in the housing area.
- Lack of proper bedding.
- Overstraining of the body.

- Undesirable walking surface.

Rumen acidosis

- This is one of the primary contributing factors to laminitis.

- It is caused by the ingestion of more carbohydrates than the rumen can ferment.

- Fiber digestion is reduced and the production of lactic acid increases.

- When the amount of fermentable carbohydrates in the food increases, the amount of rumen bacteria also goes up, producing a lot of fatty acids.

- Eventually, the pH of the rumen reduces affecting the bacterial population negatively, leading them to diminish.

- When pH is below 5, the amount of lactic acid produced increases. This leads to acidosis.

- This, in turn triggers the release of several endotoxins that leads to histamine release.

- Eventually, the lamina is destroyed, hoof deteriorates and laminitis occurs.

- Histamine is normally released when the goat is stressed. So it is possible that even environmental stress and an infection may lead to rumen acidosis.

Acute laminitis

- Systemic illness is noticed in case of acute laminitis.

- The corium is very evidently inflamed.

- The condition may recur if the metabolism rate is not restored.

- Swelling and an increase in body temperature is the first sign of acute laminitis.

- You will also notice a coronary band in the area that consists of the soft tissue.

Subclinical laminitis

- Inflammation leads to hemorrhaging eventually.
- The horn tissue grows and the hemorrhage moves quickly to the surface.
- The sole is normally 0.4 inches thick. As the hemorrhage rises, the thickness increases by 0.2 inches each month.
- This is why the hemorrhage is only noticed about two months after the infection.
- If you notice these sole hemorrhages and any yellow colouration of the hoof, the condition could be rampant in the herd.

Other diseases

There are several other diseases that affect goats particularly. Here are a few that you will have to watch out for in order to keep your pet safe from any chance of infection.

Respiratory diseases

- Also known as shipping fever, this is a type of pneumonia that is caused when the kids have been shipped.
- There are several other factors that can lead to this condition.
- Stress related to weaning, weather changes and shipping will make the goat susceptible to these infections.
- It is natural for the goat to feel some stress when they are made to travel. However, this can be managed by handling them carefully and keeping the conditions within the shipping vehicle sanitary.
- Vaccination is the best preventive measure against this condition.
- Make sure that the billy is vaccinated when he is very young. If not, they will not be able to survive should they contract this disease.

Backleg disease

- The medical term for this condition is clostridial disease.
- While there are over 60 strains of clostridial bacteria, not all of them will cause the condition in goats.

- This condition is more common in goats that are younger than 2 years of age. A gangrene formed in the muscle is the main reason for this infection.

- When the young billy does not get ample colostrum, this disease may occur.

- In older livestock, it is the result of the contamination of the vaccination needle.

Bovine respiratory syncytial virus

- This condition can be fatal in livestock at times.

- It is normally caused due to stress and may lead to severe disease of the respiratory system.

- It will also compromise the immunity of the animal against several other diseases.

- The common symptoms include runny nose and a high fever.

Viral Diarrhea

- This is one of the most expensive diseases contracted by livestock.

- The common signs are nasal discharge, fever, coughing and scurs.

- The more severe form of this disease is known as Type 2 Bovine Viral Diarrhea.

- It leads to hemorrhaging in young kids and can also lead to severe infections in the adults.

Rhinotracheitis

- This is a mild respiratory disease that often compromises the immunity of the animal.

- It is dangerous as it opens up the possibility of several other infections and diseases.

- The virus is shed through discharge in the eyes and the nose.

- In non-vaccinated animals, infections can be caused through the nasal passage and the mouth.

Haemophilus Somnus

- This is a type of bacterial infection that can lead to a series of neurological, reproductive and respiratory diseases in the goat.

- The common signs are rapid breathing, inflammation of the nasal passage, deep cough and a loss of appetite.

The best thing about goats is that they can heal wonderfully when you provide them with the right type of care and medical attention. The best way to control any infection in your pet and within your herd, if you have one, is to practice good husbandry and provide the animal with a stress free environment.

3. Finding the right vet

When you bring a Nigerian dwarf goat home, the first thing that you need to do is look for a vet. Do not wait until there is an emergency to look for one. The thing with livestock is that the vet should be specialized to deal with farm animals. There are fewer specialized vets who are already working with a large base of farms. So, looking for one near you and one who is conveniently accessible is a challenge.

Besides finding a vet, it is good for you to build a good rapport with your vet before you actually bring your dwarf home.

If your vet is familiar with your property and farm area, he will be able to make better recommendations to get your Nigerian dwarf goat into an effective healthcare regimen. They will also be able to come over in case of any emergency after your pet has been transported from the breeder to your home.

In areas where there aren't too many farms, it is harder to find a livestock vet. With the vets that are available, it is possible that they are already taking care of a large part of the livestock in that area. So, the earlier you build a rapport, the easier it will be to seek assistance when it is really needed.

Even if the vet is unable to visit the animal, he will be able to give you necessary advice on the phone in case of an emergency. Of course, the better the relationship, the more you can count on getting the right assistance even if it is in the middle of the night.

There are a few reliable sources that you can choose to get recommendations for a local livestock vet. To begin with you can check with the Cooperative

Extension office in your area where you normally purchase food and other supplies for your pet.

They can recommend specialized vets and also one who will be willing to visit your farm when needed. You can call the Cooperative Extension office and ask them for the current list of veterinarians.

Alternatively, you can even check the website of the USDA or its counterpart in other countries for a list of the closest extension office so that you can get all the information that you need on livestock vets.

There are several other experts who can help you with healthcare for your beloved pet. For instance, in a cooperative office, you should be able to find nutrition specialists. They can also give you some technical assistance when needed.

The other reliable source to get leads into local livestock vets is another farm owner. It does not matter if they own a dwarf or not. They will definitely be able to get you in touch with a vet who takes care of their livestock. This may include goats, chickens or any other farm animal or bird. Word of mouth is, in fact, the most reliable source.

If you live near a state university or college that has a veterinary division, you can also check with them for leads. In some cases they may have a hospital and clinic in house that will work perfectly in case of an emergency. Some specialists will also make farm visits when necessary, provided you are within a limited distance from the clinic.

When you are looking for a vet, there are some characteristics that will make you work well with your vet.

- The vet follows the same ideals that you do when it comes to raising your dwarf.

- Of course, you have to be flexible in your values. There are some factors that cannot change. For instance if you prefer to grass feed your dwarf, your vet must also be in favor of it.

- However, there may be times when you and your vet may not have the same logic or ideas. That is alright as long as they are respectful of your principles and are willing to work around it.

- When it comes to the welfare of your pet, you must also be willing to accept some advice from the vet even if it is not exactly what you believe in. For example, in some cases, you may have to switch to grain feed for an antibiotic to work better.

- In these cases, you can ask your vet why a certain method is better than the other. This will give you extra knowledge about your dwarf as well.

Once you have found a vet who is conveniently located and is comfortable to work with, you can ask the following questions to be entirely sure of the choice you make:

- What are your working hours?
- What equipment and livestock diagnostic resources are available with you?
- Are you available for emergencies?
- In case of an emergency, if the vet is not available, who will cover for them?
- What are the payment options?
- What is the regular fee per visit?
- Is there an additional charge to make a farm visit? If so, what are the charges?
- How can one contact the vet in case of an emergency?

There are several tips that you can take from your vet to provide first aid in case of an emergency. However, when the condition is serious, you should be able to call your vet who has all the skills to restore the health of your goat.

4. Vaccination

With the severity of infection in Nigerian dwarf goats and the rapid onset of the condition, there is no option but to take all the preventive measures possible to ensure that your pet is safe and in perfect health.

Vaccinating your goat is the best, and the most effective preventive measure against most diseases. If you are running a business with goats, it is especially important to vaccinate the animal to make your business more sustainable.

At the minimum, you must vaccinate your goat against *clostridium perfringens and tetanus*. However, most goat owners neglect this important part of goat care.

You must vaccinate your goat because:

- Deadly diseases may be prevented
- In case of any infection despite the vaccination, it is less severe and is shorter.
- Death is preventable if your goat is vaccinated.
- It's cheaper than replacing a goat or having a mass outbreak in your herd.

The first step is to make sure that disease resistance is high in your dwarf. This can be taken care of by providing good nutrition and plenty of fresh and clean water. Livestock rely extensively on the pasture that they graze on for food as well as shelter. You will have to constantly keep a check on the quality and the quantity of grass available in your pasture.

The more important thing is to make sure that you keep the grazing area free from any debris. Sadly, people tend to throw food wrappers, drink cans and bottles out in open areas without a second thought. If any of this garbage blows into the pasture, your goat may end up eating it. As discussed, the blockage is only surgically manageable.

It is a good idea to walk the line of the fence every day to check for loose wires, any debris and also to check the safety of the fence that you have put up.

Vaccination is a must against all major diseases such as anthrax. You can contact your vet for a list of vaccines that are recommended for your goat. You can also contact the cooperative extension in your area to find out what vaccination is necessary for any localized illness.

The vaccination schedule must be accurate and you need to ensure that you always get the boosters in time. Worming is also recommended to prevent several health issues in your goat.

You can obtain a computerized system that will help you maintain records and track your herd's health on a schedule. You can check the weight and even figures like the sale price of a certain member of your herd. When you want to change the composition of a herd or want to include a new member, these programs will give you a lot of data.

You must also invest in proper handling material such as harnesses and also proper transport to ensure that there is no hassle when you have to make a routine visit to the vet or when your vet comes over for a checkup.

There are two aspects of preventive care: Pasture management and herd management. Here are some tips that will help you take care of each one correctly.

5. First aid

There are a lot of simple measures that you can take to provide immediate care in case of injuries and emergencies. Knowing how you can care for your Nigerian dwarf goat is the first step to being a good owner. In some cases, it may be too late before the vet arrives or you take your goat to the vet.

Injuries in case of animals never take place in a location or time that is convenient. If you are able to take care of the injury immediately with appropriate care, you can reduce the impact of any injury.

There are a few simple principles that you can apply in each scenario with your pet. Being prepared is to have all the knowledge that is needed along with the right first aid kit. Make sure you consult your vet and learn more skills to take care of your pet.

When the animal is injured, their behavior will be very different from normal. They may not be as calm and docile as you expect them to be, so be careful when you handle an injured animal.

The first thing that you need to do is restrain the animal using a harness. When your goat is restrained properly, it will prevent further injuries to the animal and will also keep you safe.

Here are some of the common issues that you must watch out for:

Cuts, puncture wounds and scrapes

- Wash the wound with a gentle cleanser, running water or saline solution.
- If there is any debris or dirt in the wound, use a lot of saline to flush it out of the wound.
- It helps to use a large syringe or bore needle to wash the area so that you can clean the specific area.
- Even the eyewash that you use with contacts can be used to wash wounds. You can get a large container of this if needed.
- Cover the wound with some water soluble ointments and also antiseptics.

- With water soluble ointments, you will have faster results in comparison to sprays that will make the tissue dry.
- On superficial wounds, you can use an ointment that is petroleum jelly based. These ointments are not recommended when they have a certain chemical composition.

Eye injuries

- If there is any foreign object lodged in the eye it can be washed out with saline that is maintained at body temperature.
- In case you are unable to restrain a goat with eye injuries, your vet may have to tranquilize her before you do anything.
- The eyes are extremely delicate and you must make sure that you do not treat the injury unless you have adequate experience.
- In case of head and eye injuries, you and the animal can be injured severely without necessary precautions.

Bleeding

- Any form of bleeding can be controlled if you can hold the area down with gauze sponges.
- Make sure that the gauze is kept in place while you bandage it snugly enough to clot the blood but not so tight that it would restrict blood flow.
- If you are unable to control blood flow with this technique, you must call your vet immediately. This may require surgical correction.
- You can use blood stopper powder only on superficial wounds. However, these products should ever be used on deep wounds.
- If deep wounds are not treated properly, there can be tissue damage, scarring or formation of abscesses.

Hoof care

- The hoof of your goat will present several special challenges.
- Any wound in the hoof must be flushed out immediately.

- For most hoof injuries, it is best to just wash the hoof and house the animal in a dry environment.

- An absorbent wrap can be used to cover the wound. Many farms use disposable diapers as effective covers for these wounds. If not you can even use cotton.

- If you are using an elastic wrap, make sure that it is not too tight, restricting the flow of blood.

Bloating and frothy bloat

- This is common in ruminants.

- It is usually caused when the forage consists of an excessive amount of succulent legumes.

- You can use commercial products like BloatGuard to break the froth down. Vegetable oil can be used in a small quantity as a reliable home remedy.

- If the animal has free gas bloat, a speculum with a garden hose is normally used.

- In extreme cases, the vet will use a bloat trochar.

Handy first aid kit for your goat

Having the right tools and equipment in place can be a life saver in case of an emergency. When you have a Nigerian dwarf goat in your home, you can make a first aid kit on your own with the following items:

- Heavy duty scissors
- Flashlight
- Needle nosed plier
- Halter and rope
- Wire cutters
- Disposable gloves
- Skin cleanser
- Gauze sponges

- Sterile saline solution
- Water soluble ointment
- Frothy bloat equipment
- Medical tape or duct tape
- Fly repellant
- Large syringes
- Antibiotic eye ointment
- Thermometer
- Rolled cotton
- Calcium gel or calcium borogluconate
- Mineral oil
- A small dose of epinephrine
- Hoof nippers
- A knife
- A small container
- Water based lubricant
- Phone numbers of your vet, state vet and any emergency facility

It is recommended that you have your goat checked by your vet on a regular basis. It is true that medical expenses for your goat can be high. That is an important factor to keep in mind. You can also speak with insurance companies to help you find a plan that can cover your goat in case of any major procedure.

Chapter 8: Grooming the Nigerian dwarf goat

When you decide to keep a Nigerian dwarf goat as a pet, you should understand that you will have to pay attention to the basic cleaning and grooming of the Nigerian dwarf goat. This is essential to keep the Nigerian dwarf goat clean and healthy. Not only will your Nigerian dwarf goat appear neat and clean, he will also be saved from many unwanted diseases.

If you are just raising goats on a farm as part of your green lifestyle, grooming them is not that essential. On the other hand, if you are looking at showing your goat at exhibitions and animal shows, you must pay closer attention to grooming.

When you are looking at grooming sessions for your Nigerian dwarf goat, you should pay special attention to the Nigerian dwarf goat's ears, nails, teeth and its bathing. This chapter will help you to understand the various dos and don'ts while grooming your pet Nigerian dwarf goat.

Sanitation is the key to good husbandry. You need to ensure that your pet is clean and well-groomed. Nigerian dwarf goats tend to have an unpleasant odor when they are cleaned regularly.

1. Bathing your goat

A good bath is needed to make sure that there is no dirt or manure on your goat's body. Of course, this needs to be done carefully to prevent startling the animal, leading to unpleasant situations. A regular bath can prevent possible infections in the skin and also the chances of any parasites affecting the health of the animal.

Here are a few steps that will help you keep your goat clean in the most effortless way:

If you do not have access to warm water to bathe your goat with, make sure that you wait for a warm day to carry this out. Goats tend to be very unpleasant when they are washed in cold conditions. They will display bad behavior all day long.

The first thing you need to do is secure the goat using a rope or a halter that is fastened to a collar. The best option is to tie your dwarf to the side of a wall or the building. Using a pole to fasten the goat will lead to her walking around in circles. The rope that you choose should not be more than 1.5 feet in length. That way, your goat can eat some grass or hay when you are bathing her, but will not get too much room to move around. A shorter rope is recommended if this is the first bath you are giving your goat or if she is known to misbehave during a bath.

The knot that you use to secure the animal should be easy to release. That way, in case of a tangle or a fall, you can release the goat safely.

Wet the whole body of the goat starting from the legs and then working your way up to the back. Make sure that you are cautious in the beginning as the reaction of the goat to water is unpredictable. The area around the head and face should be cleaned in the end to make sure that you do not get any soap or water in the ears and eyes.

It is common for goats to have mud or manure stuck on the hair. You will face this issue more often with long haired dwarfs. If there are large chunks you may have to carefully cut it out without making the coat seem different.

If you have a pressure washer, it will come quite handy when it comes to removing dirt from the tail or the legs. The water acts like a comb to remove this dirt from the hair. Make sure that the power washer does not hurt your goat. This means that it should not be used on sensitive areas like the face, belly and the udder.

You need to use soap on your goat to get her fully clean. Soap up one side at a time. Then you can move to the feet and the legs. The best option is baby shampoo. You can also consult your vet to provide special soap that can improve the condition of the hair and the skin. Using your hand is good enough for most areas. A hard brush is needed on the legs and the back to remove any dirt.

The soap must be rinsed off fully. To do this start at the backline and then move down to the legs. Make sure that you do not leave any soap on the body as the chemicals can cause skin problems.

Don't let the goat into the housing area. Let her walk around in the sun and dry off fully. You do not want hay and other material sticking to the wet hair, making your efforts go in vain.

Be patient with the goat. If there is a lot of squirming, allow her to settle down before you wash her. If you have a large pond that you can lure her into, it is the easiest option to give her a nice and clean bath.

2. Hair trimming

Clipping your goat's hair annually is extremely beneficial to the animals. It also reduces the maintenance efforts on your part. An annual clip is best recommended as it helps keep the hair of the goats short enough for the rest of the year.

There are battery powered and electrical clippers that are available in most pet stores. If you are using these electrical clippers, you need to make sure that you check them frequently to ensure that they are not too hot. You will also have to spray the goat's body with water or cooling oil as required. The clippers need to be cleaned and piled as needed.

It is easier to clip the goat's hair if you wash the goat just before you clip the hair. Many doe owners like to clip off the beard. However, clipping any area on the face is recommended only if you are planning to sow your goat. Otherwise, it is a real challenge.

When you are trimming the body of the goat, it is a good idea to use a 10 blade trimmer. Start from the top of the body and start trimming against the fur of your goat. Next, you need to use smooth and long motions to make sure that the hair doesn't look choppy and chunky. You need to move the skin over the hip and other bony areas to make sure that the cut is smooth.

Next you need to clip the hair from the neck, leg, chest, back and sides. The best way is to clip the areas with longer hair first and then move to the areas with shorter hair. If you want to correct the trimming, you can just move the trimmer with short strokes.

When you are trimming the hair on the udder and belly, you need to be really careful. Use a 30 to 40 blade trimmer for this. Clip the middle of the belly till the area between the legs. Then when you are clearing the area around the udder, lift the legs and do so. As you clear the udder, hold the teats between your thumb and two fingers to make sure you don't nick the area.

You would have noticed hair that is hanging over the hooves. Make sure you trim this hair. To add the finishing touch, brush off any excess hair and then trim any uneven areas.

After you have finished clipping the hair of your goat, if you notice any area that is very exposed, you can rub some corn starch over it to avoid sunburns.

3. Hoof trimming

Lameness in goats is a very common issue. There are several factors that contribute and may be interrelated in some cases. But one of the main reasons why goats have hoof related issues is when the hoof is uneven. That leads to an unbalanced weight on the legs causing issues with the one that is carrying most of the weight.

If one hoof is being overloaded, it will become sensitive, prone to lameness and very unstable. Make sure that you check the hooves of your goat regularly and trim them for two reasons:

- In order to restore the weight balance on all four hooves equally.
- To check for any possible lesions in the hooves.

You need to examine the goat and make sure that trimming is required. If you over-trim you can put the goat at a risk for walking issues.

There are four steps in a good claw trimming process. Make sure that every foot is approached with this technique. This will avoid over trimming. It is recommended that you seek the assistance of someone with experience before you try to do this on your own.

Step 1: Measuring toe length

- The measurement will begin at the hairline to the tip of the toe. This is called the front wall. You will measure the inside claw present on the hind feet.
- If the claw length is more than 3 inches, it should be removed. You will make a cut that is perpendicular to the sole. When you do so, the toe will have a square end.
- The inside claw on the hind feet must be trimmed first. Then proceed to the other claws to make sure that they match. This is the same process with the front legs but you will start from the outer claw.

Step 2: Maintain the thickness of the sole

- The thickness of the sole at the toe and the length of the claw are directly correlated. The thickness of the sole will be measured from the tip of the toe that you just cut. If the thickness is more than 0.25 inches, you can reduce the thickness.

- When you trim the sole, start from the front and move to the back. The horn on the hind claw should not be removed. The sole thickness should be maintained at 0.25 inches from the tip of the toe.

- The claws that are less than 3 inches should not be trimmed. You must also never trim any hoof with a sole thickness that is less than 0.25 inches.

- In most cases you will only have to trim the outside of your rear claw. That way you will be able restore balance and remove overgrowth if any.

- When you apply pressure on the sole, it should not seem flexible after trimming.

Step 3: Measure the depth of the heel

- You can measure the depth of the heel from the bottom of the sole to just below the hairline. This measurement should be taken on the outside of the claw or the heel wall juncture.

- If you see that the measurement is more than more than 1.5 inches, you should trim the horn from that heel.

- Usually, heel depth is low in goats that are housed in an area with a concrete floor.

Step 4: Maintain claw and heel balance

- The surface between the inner and outer surface should be flat and capable of bearing weight after you are done with the trimming process.

- The sole will not be trimmed if you feel that it flexes when you apply pressure with your thumb or finger.

- The heel and claw balance should be checked. For this, you can use the front walls of both legs and place them on a flat surface that will go across both heels and both the toes. It should also be measured from the toe to the heel on both feet. If you can see some light from below the flat surface, it means that you have to check the trim that you have made.

You will get a special hoof trimmer in any pet store. You can also order online or buy one from the vet. These trimmers are very similar to the nail file that we use in our homes to remove any excess growth.

If you feel confident, you can go through with this. However, during your first attempt, you can have someone with experience accompany you. You may even seek the assistance of your vet if you feel like it is a difficult task for you.

When trimmed improperly, the goat struggles to gain balance when walking or just standing. If you over trim, the animal may feel a lot of pain and is also susceptible to several injuries. Make sure that you have a step by step approach that allows the animal to calm down fully before you try to trim the hoof.

4. Grooming of other parts

There are some basic grooming routines that you must include. We will discuss some of them in more detail in the following section.

Brushing

This is one of the most beneficial grooming routines, as it can remove any loose hair or dandruff. That helps improve the quality of your goat's skin and coat. The circulation of blood also increases and you can check for any signs of illness such as swelling, lumps or abscesses.

It is recommended to brush goats during early summer or late spring when they actually begin to shed the undercoat that they needed during winter. You will get special firm bristled brushes in pet stores.

Clipping of the tail

Before and after the birth of a kid, there are several fluids that get stuck to the tail of the doe and the area around it. So, clip up the sides of the tail all the way to the end of the tail to make it short.

Clipping of the udder

Clipping your goats annually is a great idea. If the hair is shorter, the goats are able to stay cooler. There is also more sunlight on their skin, keeping lice and other parasites at bay. The best time to clip your goat's hair is a day or two after winter is fully over. Make sure you remove the hair on the belly and around the udder. This is important to make sure that the hair does not fall into the milk.

Chapter 9: Training the Nigerian dwarf goat

It is very important to train the animal to make him more suitable to a household. By nature, Nigerian dwarf goats can be a little naughty. You will have to train them to tame them.

Like training most other animals, Nigerian dwarf goat training will also require you to be patient. You will have to do a few trial and errors before you can be sure that your Nigerian dwarf goat is well trained. You should remember to have fun even during the training phase.

The training phase can be a great opportunity for you to learn more about your little pet. No matter how much you read about a Nigerian dwarf goat, your pet will have some individual properties that will separate him from the rest of the lot. This is a good time to learn about all these properties.

The more you learn about your pet, the stronger bond you form with him. You should remember to not take the training phase as a cumbersome thing. In fact, take it as an opportunity to form an everlasting bond with your pet. Your pet will also understand you better during this time.

While you have to be thorough during this phase, you should not be harsh and rude. Don't beat the Nigerian dwarf goat and terrorize. You will only scare the pet and jeopardize your relationship with him.

If you have your doubts, it is better to read more about them and then take your decisions regarding the Nigerian dwarf goat's training phase.

1. Training your dwarf goat

While not many people think of goat, regular or miniature, as pets, the truth is that they can be a lot of fun to be around. Nigerian dwarf goats are very playful and their small size also makes them more approachable.

Now that you have learnt all about approaching the goat correctly, the next step is to train them. Goats and kids can be trained for shows and also to run errands on your farm. This training practice makes the bond between the owner and the goat a lot stronger, as it has the potential to build a lot of trust.

Halter training

This is a very important type of training if you want to present your Nigerian dwarf goat or billy in livestock shows. Also known as halter breaking, this process is time consuming and requires a lot of patience and persistence from your end. Irrespective of the breed that you have, it is best that you start this training when the goat is very young.

The advantage is that you will be able to handle a billy better than an adult who is much stronger. Halter training a goat is very similar to a horse. Of course, the behavior of the two animals is quite different which means that you have to change your approach quite a bit.

When you are halter training livestock, the methods differ based on the age and the size of the animal. It is easier to get a billy on a halter and lead him around for a while. In the case of older animals, they will take some time to get used to the halter and will also need to understand what you really expect from them.

Typically, a billy that has been weaned from the mother recently is the easiest to halter train.

The technique mentioned in this section is effective in the younger kids and the older ones. The method itself was devised for livestock that are still not of the weaning age, that is, about 6 months of age. However, it works equally well on livestock of all breeds and ages.

Catching the billy

The first step is to get hold of the billy that you want to train. Leading them into a smaller enclosure is a good idea as they will not have too much space to run away from you.

If the billy is just a few days old, they tend to be a little dopey. That means that you can lead the billy to a corner and then get hold of him. The mother should not be around, especially if she is not halter trained herself. She will show you signs of discomfort when you begin to corner the billy and try to get a lasso around the neck so that you can lead them to halter training.

When they are older than a week, it is harder to catch the billy. However, if you learn how to approach them calmly without startling them, you will be able to get a lasso around the neck quite easily. Using this lasso, you can lead the billy to the part of the farm where you wish to have the halter on him.

That said, be prepared for a lot of resistance when you try to pull a billy by the neck using a lasso. They will try to break free as quickly as possible and will put up quite the fight. Wait for the billy to settle down and take a few steps forward. Do this till he is walking comfortably with you.

Now if your kids have been bottle fed, they are most likely used to the presence of human beings. In that case, the protest will be absent and you will also find it very easy to catch the billy. All you have to do is present the bottle that you feed him from and he will walk towards you voluntarily.

Getting the halter on

When you have successfully lead the billy to the area that you want to halter him in, you can begin to do so while you keep a strong grip on the rope that you used to lead him.

The halter will go over the head and the ears first before going over the nose. The ears should be looped through the halter to make it fit comfortably. A rope halter will have an adjustable portion that will go on the nose. You will keep it as wide open as possible when you get the nose of the livestock into it. Then, you can tighten the rope around the muzzle.

You also have the option of using a leather halter that will go on the same way as a rope halter. Make sure that the head piece is snug but not so tight that it pinches the muzzle. Use a non-show halter to begin with.

If the billy has been unruly in the past or if you are dealing with an older goat, having a head gate installed is a good idea. That way, there is no chance of the billy running away when you are just half way through getting the halter on. You also will be able to prevent any injury to yourself if the billy or older goat is unhappy with the halter and reacts in a negative manner.

Following this you can connect the lead onto the metal ring that is present on a leather halter. With a rope halter, you do not have to add a lead as it already comes with a rope that is attached to the halter.

Once this is done, the halter should be left on for a few days, preferably a week. That way, the billy gets used to the halter and will also understand the amount of pressure that is applied on the halter in case he accidentally steps on it. You will move on to the next step only when the billy is comfortable with the halter.

Stay close to the billy

This should be done especially if you are not bottle feeding the goat. That will help him get used to your presence. You can give him range cubes and other treats when you are around. Hand feeding is recommended as that will encourage the billy to approach you comfortably. If your billy is not particularly fond of range cubes, you can even offer some grain from your hand. The goal is to get him to approach you rather than you having to corner him or chase him around to catch him.

Keep the housing area of the billy extremely clean and make sure that he is not in a crowded area in the resting area. The lesser the stress, the better the response to halter training. You must also talk to him in a calm voice at all times.

The next step is to practice tying the billy using the halter lead. Make a few loops of the lead around a post and then tie a knot. That will keep it sturdy and will prevent the billy from breaking loose. The distance between the post and the head of the billy should not be more than 12 inches.

The first time you tie the billy, keep him there for not more than 30 minutes. As he gets used to it, you may increase the time being tied. When the billy is tied up, stroke his chin or ears to make him feel relaxed. This will also lead to positive associations with you in the future.

Using the lead

The next step from there is to actually get the billy to walk on a lead. Hold the lead in your hand and keep it short in length. Slowly walk forward and encourage the billy to do the same.

You must stay on the left side of the billy. Never allow the billy to lead. You must stay ahead. If the billy tries to step ahead of you, just stop, collect the billy and start only after he is beside you.

Never drag the billy along as you walk. Pull gently and encourage the billy to walk. When he begins to walk, just release the lead a little. You will do this till the billy learns to walk next to you. It may take several attempts. So, be patient.

Then, you can start turning when you are walking the billy on the lead. You have to watch out for any signs of protests such as jumping or pulling back. If this happens, calm down, get the billy beside you and then continue with the training. Try not to let go and keep a strong grip on the lead.

In an event that the billy escapes, catch him calmly using the methods mentioned above. Once that is done, you will continue to train. The training session will always end on your terms.

If not, he will pick up bad habits like pulling. The more you practice, the better you will get at leading the goat using a halter.

2. Training goats to pack

Once you have trained your goat to follow your lead, you can also take him with you on hikes. They are great for backpacking. When you plan to take your goats on hikes, they must be trained for the following:

- Your goats must get used to being tied. When you go on camps, the goats will be tied when you are resting. For this you will need a leash and a sturdy collar. Start by tying the goat to a fence and observing him. If he begins to get restless and tangles himself in the leash, just untangle him. As he gets used to this concept, increase the time that you keep him tied up for.

- Your goat must follow your lead. This will happen only when you leash train him completely.

- They must learn to stand as well. There will be several instances when your goats will have to stand during the trial. This means that your goat must learn to stop when you halt. This is possible only when he is trained regularly.

- They must also get used to wearing the pannier that they will carry stuff in. You can start by allowing the goat to examine the pannier. Then, saddle it on the back with a gap for two fingers between the body and the cinch strap of the saddle.

3. How to make the goat cooperate

There is a step by step approach to make sure that your goat is cooperative throughout the process. This takes some practice and dedication from your end.

You need to have a separate enclosure that is clean and sanitized for milking. The goal is to have the goat trot in comfortably when you open the door.

Keep the goat tethered

The lesser the movement of the goat, the easier it is. When you tether the goat, here are a few things that you need to do:

- The goat must be tethered such that her head faces a wall. Having a metal ring or a rod on the wall will help you do this easily. A ring is a better option as it will allow the head to move up and down.

- The lead that you have on the harness is the best option. Tie one end to the ring or rod, keeping the lead short.

- The goat should not be able to move her head from side to side. When the ring moves, she will be able to bend down and reach for the food. The goat will be able to see you from the side and will have an idea about what is going on. That will help him remain calm throughout.

4. Advanced training for goats

As your goat is accustomed to interacting with you, you may teach him more complicated tricks. You need a lot of patience for this and you must spend several hours with your pet goats to be successful. There are two things with advanced training:

Clicker training

Goats can be taught just about any trick in the book using a clicker. A clicker is a mechanical device that you will find in most pet stores. This device makes a long clicking sound and when combined with treats like peanuts, it is an excellent training aid.

The sound of the clicker with the treat tells the goat that he is doing something right. For this, you need to make that connection between the treat and the clicker.

To establish this, make a sound with the clicker and give the goat a treat about 30 times. This will make the goat respond to the clicker as it would respond to a treat.

The next step is to start training the goat. Use a cue word such as "come". When the goat does what you expect it to, just click. If he completes the task, add a bonus and give him a treat.

The goat will learn to respond to commands with a lot of practice. When you are teaching more complicated tricks, break them down and teach each step using a clicker.

The obstacle course: If you want to show your goat, you must make sure that you teach him to complete an obstacle course. You can use a clicker and treats to train your goat.

When you create the obstacle course, be creative. Use steps, hoops and even old tires. Anything that the goat can climb or go through may be used.

Conclusion

Thank you again for purchasing this book.

I hope this book was able to help you in understanding the various ways to domesticate and care for Nigerian dwarf goats.

Nigerian dwarf goats are adorable and lovable animals. These animals have been domesticated for many years. Even though they are loved as pets, they are not very common, and there are still many doubts regarding their domestications methods and techniques. There are many things that the prospective owners don't understand about the animal. They find themselves getting confused as to what should be done and what should be avoided.

A Nigerian dwarf goat is a small naughty animal that will keep you busy and entertained by all its unique antics and mischiefs. It is said that each animal is different from the other. Each one will have some traits that are unique to him. It is important to understand the traits that differentiate the Nigerian dwarf goat from other animals. You also have to be sure that you can provide for the animal. So, it is important to be acquainted with the dos and don'ts of keeping the Nigerian dwarf goat.

If you wish to raise a Nigerian dwarf goat as a pet, there are many things that you need to understand before you can domesticate the animal. You need to make sure that you are ready in terms of right preparation. There are certain unique characteristics of the animal that make him adorable, but these traits can also be very confusing for many people. You can't domesticate the animal with all the confusions in your head.

If you are still contemplating whether you want to domesticate the Nigerian dwarf goat or not, then it becomes all the more important for you to understand everything regarding the pet very well. When you are planning to domesticate a Nigerian dwarf goat as a pet, you should lay special emphasis on learning about its behaviour, habitat requirements, diet requirements and common health issues.

When you decide to domesticate an animal, it is important that you understand the animal and its species well. It is important to learn the basic nature and mannerisms of the animal. This book will help you to equip yourself with this knowledge. You will be able to appreciate the Nigerian dwarf goats for what they are. You will also know what to expect from the animal. This will help you to decide whether the Nigerian dwarf goat is the right choice for you or not. If you already have a Nigerian dwarf goat, then this book will help you to strengthen your bond with your pet.

The ways and strategies discussed in the book are meant to help you get acquainted with everything that you need to know about Nigerian dwarf goats. You will be able to understand the unique antics of the animal. This will help you to decide whether the Nigerian dwarf goat is suitable to be your pet. The book teaches you simple ways that will help you to understand your pet. This will allow you take care of your pet in a better way. You should be able to appreciate your pet and also care well for the animal with the help of the techniques discussed in this book.

Thank you and good luck.

References

Note: at the time of printing, all the websites below were working. As the internet changes rapidly, some sites might no longer be live when you read this book. That is, of course, out of our control.

https://en.wikipedia.org

https://www.lovethatpet.com

http://www.Nigerian dwarf goat-world.com

https://www.thespruce.com

https://www.bluecross.org.uk

http://www.seniorlink.co.nz

https://www.cuteness.com

http://www.arkive.org

http://www.vetstreet.com

www.training.ntwc.org

www.wildlifehealth.org

http://animaldiversity.org

https://www.yourpetspace.info

http://healthypets.mercola.com

https://www.finecomb.com

https://a-z-animals.com

https://www.theguardian.com

http://www.marshallpet.com

https://www.all-about-Nigerian dwarf goats.com

Copyright and Trademarks: This publication is Copyrighted 2018 by Zoodoo Publishing. All products, publications, software and services mentioned and recommended in this publication are protected by trademarks. In such instance, all trademarks & copyright belong to the respective owners. All rights reserved. No part of this book may be reproduced or transferred in any form or by any means, graphic, electronic, or mechanical, including photocopying, recording, taping, or by any information storage retrieval system, without the written permission of the authors. Pictures used in this book are either royalty free pictures bought from stock-photo websites or have the source mentioned underneath the picture.

Disclaimer and Legal Notice: This product is not legal or medical advice and should not be interpreted in that manner. You need to do your own due-diligence to determine if the content of this product is right for you. The author and the affiliates of this product are not liable for any damages or losses associated with the content in this product. While every attempt has been made to verify the information shared in this publication, neither the author nor the affiliates assume any responsibility for errors, omissions or contrary interpretation of the subject matter herein. Any perceived slights to any specific person(s) or organization(s) are purely unintentional. We have no control over the nature, content and availability of the web sites listed in this book. The inclusion of any web site links does not necessarily imply a recommendation or endorse the views expressed within them. Zoodoo Publishing takes no responsibility for, and will not be liable for, the websites being temporarily unavailable or being removed from the Internet. The accuracy and completeness of information provided herein and opinions stated herein are not guaranteed or warranted to produce any particular results, and the advice and strategies, contained herein may not be suitable for every individual. The author shall not be liable for any loss incurred as a consequence of the use and application, directly or indirectly, of any information presented in this work. This publication is designed to provide information in regards to the subject matter covered. The information included in this book has been compiled to give an overview of the subject s and detail some of the symptoms, treatments etc. that are available to people with this condition. It is not intended to give medical advice. For a firm diagnosis of your condition, and for a treatment plan suitable for you, you should consult your doctor or consultant. The writer of this book and the publisher are not responsible for any damages or negative consequences following any of the treatments or methods highlighted in this book. Website links are for informational purposes and should not be seen as a personal endorsement; the same applies to the products detailed in this book. The reader should also be aware that although the web links included were correct at the time of writing, they may become out of date in the future.

www.ingramcontent.com/pod-product-compliance
Lightning Source LLC
Chambersburg PA
CBHW061451040426
42450CB00007B/1317